Daniel Maselli; Beat Sottas (eds.)

Research Partnerships for Common Concerns

Proceedings of the
International Conference on

Scientific Research Partnership
for Sustainable Development

North-South and South-South Dimensions,
Berne, March 5–7, 1996

Daniel Maselli; Beat Sottas (eds.)

Research Partnerships for Common Concerns

Proceedings of the
International Conference on

Scientific Research Partnership for Sustainable Development

North-South and South-South Dimensions,
Berne, March 5 – 7, 1996

The publication of the Proceedings has been financed by the
Swiss Commission for Research Partnerships with Developing Countries (KFPE)
Swiss Academy of Sciences (SAS), Berne
CIBA-Geigy Foundation for Co-operation with Developing Countries, Basle
Swiss Agency for Development and Co-operation (SDC), Berne

Cover designed by Allcomm Business Communications Ltd. (Allschwil, Switzerland) on a draft by Daniel Maselli

Front cover photographs by Daniel Maselli & stock-pictures from the Swiss Tropical Institute (STI, Basle) and the Swiss Agency for Development and Co-operation (SDC, Berne); back cover photographs by Christian Bobst, Zurich.

Die Deutsche Bibliothek – CIP-Einheitsaufnahme

Research Partnerships for Common Concerns :
Proceedings of the International Conference on
Scientific Research Partnership for Sustainable Development
North-South and South-South Dimensions,
Berne, March 5-7, 1996 /
Daniel Maselli; Beat Sottas (eds.) . – Hamburg : LIT, 1996
    ISBN 3-8258-2987-1

NE: GT

© LIT VERLAG
Grindelberg 15a   20144 Hamburg   Tel. 040–44 64 46   Fax 040–44 14 22

The Conference was organised by the
**Swiss Commission
for Research Partnership with Developing Countries
(KFPE)**
a Commission of the Conference of the Swiss Scientific Academies (CASS)

jointly with the

**Swiss Agency for Development and Co-operation (SDC)
Swiss Priority Programme Environment (SPPE)**
a research programme of the Swiss National Science Foundation (SNSF)
**Swiss Academy of Sciences (SAS)
Graduate Institute of Development Studies (IUED)**

Organising Committee of the Conference
Prof. Dr. Thierry A. Freyvogel (Chairman, KFPE)
Prof. Dr. Claude Auroi (IUED/EADI)
Anne-Christine Clottu Vogel (SAS)
Dr. Rudolf Häberli (SPPE)
Dr. Urs Herren (SDC)
Prof. Dr. Jean-Luc Maurer (IUED)

Executive Secretaries of the Conference
Dr. Daniel Maselli (KFPE)
&
Dr. Beat Sottas (SPPE)

Address for correspondence
KFPE
Bärenplatz 2
CH-3011 Berne, Switzerland
Tel. +41 31 311 06 01
Fax +41 31 312 16 78 / ... 32 91
e-mail: kfpe@sanw.unibe.ch

Acknowledgements for support of the Conference

The Organising Committee was most grateful for financial support for the Conference granted by:
Swiss Agency for Development and Co-operation (SDC), Berne
Swiss Priority Programme Environment (SPPE), Berne
Swiss Academy of Sciences (SAS), Berne
Swiss Academy of the Humanities and Social Sciences, Berne
Ciba-Geigy Foundation for Co-operation with Developing Countries, Basle
Swiss Academy of Technical Sciences, Zurich
Migros Co-operative Basle (Cultural Fund), Münchenstein/Basle
Swiss Society of African Studies, Berne & Geneva

The following organisations kindly contributed to the travel and accommodation expenses of participants from the South:
Federal Office of Environment, Forests and Landscape (FOEFL/BUWAL), Berne
Swiss National Science Foundation (SNSF), Berne
Swiss Tropical Institute (STI), Basle
Federal Institute of Technology, CFRC Coopération, Lausanne
University of Fribourg, Seminar of Penal Law
CIBA-Geigy Foundation for Co-operation with Developing Countries, Basle
Intercoopération (IC), Berne
University of Zurich, Rectorat & Dept. of General Linguistics, Section African Linguistics

The Organising Committee is also much indebted to the University of Berne for hosting the Conference in its buildings and to the State of Berne as well as to the City of Berne for offering the wine of honour at the reception, Tuesday March 5, 1996.

Editors' Acknowledgements

The editors are very much indebted to Prof. Thierry A. Freyvogel who helped to launch the debate and took the initiative in convening an International Conference in Switzerland on research partnership with developing countries. Over a period of more than two years he was working to develop a network among concerned people from both research programmes and development co-operation. His efforts aimed at stimulating a shift in the prevailing practices regarding research in developing countries, as proposed in the "Swiss Strategy for the Promotion of Research with Developing Countries". We are thankful for his support and guidance as the Chairman of the Organising Committee of the Conference, and for his help in elaborating a coherent and committed Swiss research policy for the future.

We should also like to thank the members of the Organising Committee - Claude Auroi (IUED/EADI), Anne-Christine Clottu Vogel (SAS), Rudolf Häberli (SPPE), Urs Herren (SDC) and Jean-Luc Maurer (IUED) - for their contributions and advice. This was given not only before and during the Conference, but in the planning and editing of the Proceedings. The Editors also appreciated the contribution of Felix Nicolier (Ciba-Geigy) as a member of the Editorial Committee.

The speakers at the Conference, too, helped in the preparation of the Proceedings by providing manuscripts and by reading and commenting on the summaries of the discussions and other contributions.

The editors decided that as well as an account of the discussions at the Conference, the Proceedings should include some chapters going beyond the Conference and looking towards the future. Special thanks go to Jacques Forster (IUED), Marcel Tanner (STI), Peter Trutmann (ZIL), Urs Herren and Adrian Hadorn (both SDC) who accepted the challenging task of writing new chapters for Part II in a very short period of time, addressing the need for a new agenda for research partnership.

For the critical reading and editing of the manuscripts the editors express their most sincere gratitude to Jennifer Jenkins and Jackie Leach Scully.

Finally, the editors would like to thank Marina Targa, Thomas Lutz and Wolfgang Hartmann for their assistance in the creation of the layout of the cover as well as Christian Bobst for the photographs taken during the Conference.

As Executive Secretaries of the Conference the editors are also very grateful to the secretariat staff and the assisting crew for their inestimable efforts before, during and after the Conference: Meret Aebi, Benjamin Bracher, Camelia Chebbi, Francesca Escher (GIUB), Manuela Gebert, Florence Guala (IUED), Silvia Hugi, Beatrice Lumbiarres (FUNDES), Claudia Maselli, Renato Marioni, David Marmet, Emma Marxer, Marion Michel, Christopher Prein, Stephan Schmidlin, Anita Scholtes, Eva Soom, Therese Stump (SDC), Myriam Von Aarburg, Andreas Witz, Dieter Wolf and Cornelia Zinsmeister.

Daniel Maselli & Beat Sottas
Berne, August 1996

Table of Contents

11 Foreword

Part I Overview

13 General Introduction
15 Summary and General Conclusions
19 Collected Recommendations

Part II State of and Perspectives in Research Partnerships

27 Needs & Concepts as seen from the South
36 Selected Statements of Representatives of the South
41 Towards a Shift in Research for Development:
    A new Agenda for Partnership
59 Promoting Research Capacities in Developing Countries
    and Countries in Transition: *The Contribution of SDC*
64 The Swiss National Science Foundation and Research for
    Development

Part III Contributions to the Conference

69 Conference Program Overview
75 Research Partnership - its Potential for Sustainable
    Development (Opening Addresses & Introductions)
89 Keynote Addresses
89 *Capacity Building in Science and Technology*
94 *The Contribution of Research to Sustainable
    Development*
101 *The Role of the World Bank*
107 *The Private Sector and Research Partnership*

113 Concepts of Research Partnership (Round Table)
119 International Competition for Research in the South - International Programmes and the Experiences of Different Partners (Panel Discussion)
128 Swiss Policy in Partnership (Forum)
137 Working Groups (Reports)

Part IV Annex

157 The Conference Participants - an Overview
159 List and Addresses of Participants
185 Poster Exhibition: List of Themes and Contact Persons
191 Selected References Touching the Domain of Research Partnership

Part I   Overview

Foreword

To prepare a Conference like the one reported on in the present Proceedings is hard work, but it has been a most rewarding exercise, too. All those concerned deserve our sincere gratitude, for to reach constructive agreements with colleagues who may look back on decades of personal experience, in greatly diverging disciplines and often in very different parts of the world, requires a great deal of open-mindedness, honesty and selflessness.

It would make little sense to list here all the people who have contributed in some way or another to the success of the Conference. They are mentioned in detail in the Editors' Acknowledgements. I wish to mention three names only. The first is that of Prof. Claude Auroi, Secretary General of the European Association of Development Research and Training Institutes (EADI); the idea of a conference on scientific research partnership was his. The others are those of our two Executive Secretaries and subsequently main Editors of these Proceedings, Dr Daniel Maselli and Dr Beat Sottas. Their enthusiasm and tenacity were essential to the success of the enterprise.

In retrospect, it may be said that, by and large, the two first aims of the Conference were attained (see p. 14). Firstly, it did succeed in calling the attention of members of the scientific community, and a number of decision-makers, to the value of research for development and the importance of partnership in research with the South. Secondly, we heard about a lot of the experience that research workers from North and South have already gained with research partnership. As to the third aim of the Conference, the implementation of equitable research co-operation, it must be kept in mind that conferences, at best, take us a little step further in the right direction. And that though such events have their place, ultimately it is not conferences which are wanted - it is research, in partnership.

Much work lies ahead. It is gratifying, though, to note that some of the recommendations made at the Conference have since been taken up. To give only two examples: the Swiss National Science Foundation (SNSF) is currently re-considering its policy with reference to research projects in and with the South (cf. Part II), and the Swiss Commission for Research Partnerships with Developing Countries (KFPE) has revised its Action Plan and is about to edit a Code of Conduct for research in partnership, with the support of the Swiss Agency for Development and Co-operation (SDC) and the Swiss Academy of Sciences (SAS). It may, finally, be mentioned that representatives of KFPE were recently invited for consultations with comparable bodies in two other European countries.

Let us have no illusions; to change people's minds and behaviour is difficult and time-consuming. Yet the message is simple. In a nutshell, the keywords of the Conference were three: more commitment; intellectual honesty, and mutual trust.

Thierry A. Freyvogel
Chairman KFPE and Organising Committee

Part I   Overview

General Introduction

In the course of the last few years three things have become increasingly clear. Firstly, without major contributions on the part of scientific research there will be no solutions to the growing worldwide problems which endanger life on earth. Secondly, research activities are needed in the South as much as in the North. Thirdly, however, in many countries in the South, the efforts undertaken so far to strengthen the research capacities have not resulted in establishing the research potential needed.

Increasing disparities between the North and the South - and the subsequent impoverishment of the South - hamper the developing countries' capacity to finance the finding of appropriate answers to crucial problems. The diminishing investment capacity of developing countries leads, among other undesired effects, to a decrease in the research capacities available. Moreover, the present global distribution of qualified researchers is inadequate, and their number insufficient. Thus, the present situation does not allow for sustainable development, either of the South or of the North.

Because of this, from 1990 to 1993 a Working Group, appointed jointly by the Swiss Agency for Development and Co-operation (SDC) and the Swiss Academy of Sciences (SAS), elaborated the *Swiss Strategy for the Promotion of Scientific Research in Developing Countries*[i]. In the most innovative section of this document the suggestion was made that international research teams be set up, composed of researchers from both South and North. Such teams would tackle problems of common interest together, on a long-term basis, in an interdisciplinary manner, and with the aim of contributing to the lasting improvement of day-to-day life in local communities of the South. Ongoing on-the-job training of all members of the teams would constitute a real empowerment with respect to the South's and the North's capacity for solving problems in the future. Subsequently, in 1995, similar proposals were taken up

also in the *Guidelines North-South - Report by the Federal Council on Switzerland's North-South Relations in the 1990s*[ii].
The "*Strategy*" created considerable interest in Switzerland, among members of the Administration as well as the scientific community. However, its authors felt that it should be scrutinised by members of the international scientific community, in particular by potential partners from the South. That was why the *International Conference on Scientific Research Partnership for Sustainable Development* was convened. Berne, the capital city of Switzerland, was chosen as the venue, because it was considered important to call the attention of both the Swiss scientific community and the policy-makers to the significance and prospects of collaborative research with the South.

It is our hope that the Proceedings of this Conference will contribute to promoting the discussion of research partnership in general, and help to put into action what was suggested during this 3 day-meeting.

Aims of the Conference

The Conveners agreed on the following three main aims:
- To call the attention of the scientific community and of decision-makers to the value of research for development and to the importance of partnership in research with and among countries in the South.
- To hear from research workers from institutions both in the South and in the North about the experience they have gained hitherto with research partnership.
- To jointly define ways in which research collaboration among dissimilar partners can be efficiently carried out, to search for new forms of institutional partnership, to enhance capacity and institution-building, as well as to create adequate follow-up mechanisms.

re-arranged from the Programme of the Conference

---

[i] obtainable from the KFPE-Secretariat, Berne
[ii] obtainable from DFAE/SDC, P.O.Box CH-3003 Berne

Summary and General Conclusions

Thierry A. Freyvogel

Setting the stage

The International Conference on Scientific Research Partnership for Sustainable Development - North-South and South-South Dimensions was held in Switzerland, at the University of Berne, from March 5-7 1996. The original proposal for the Conference came from the Institute of Development Studies in Geneva, and it was subsequently organised by a committee appointed by the Swiss Commission for Research Partnership with Developing Countries (KFPE). It was supported to a large extent by the Swiss Agency for Development and Co-operation (SDC), and was co-financed by the Swiss National Science Foundation (SNSF), the Swiss Academy of Sciences (SAS), and private foundations (see p. 6). The Conference was attended by over 370 participants, among whom were 90 colleagues from 50 countries in the South, and some 60 from 16 industrialised countries other than Switzerland (Annex). The disciplines they represented were quite diverse, ranging from agricultural engineering to history and social sciences.

The deliberations took as their starting point the Swiss Strategy for the Promotion of Research in Developing Countries (see above, General Introduction) and aimed at jointly defining ways in which research collaboration among dissimilar partners can be efficiently carried out (see Aims of the Conference, p. 14). The debates turned out to be lively and stimulating; they were characterised by frankness, open-mindedness and receptiveness. The informal side of the meeting was also very lively, and many valuable contacts were established - including new South-South acquaintanceships - many of which may prove to have long-lasting effects.

The relevance of the topic was reflected in the high attendance at the Conference, and the priority given to it in Switzerland was highlighted by the fact that Federal Councillor Flavio Cotti, Minister of Foreign Affairs for Switzerland accepted the invitation to give the Opening Address (Part III), and Ambassador Walter Fust, Director SDC, to deliver the closing one. Furthermore, members of Parliament together with high-ranking decision makers in the field of Swiss research policy agreed to participate in the Forum (Part III, Swiss Policy in Partnership).

Results

The needs for more and sustainable research in the South were contested by no one, either with reference to capacity building (Part III, especially Keynote Address Hassan) or to the contribution of scientific research to sustainable development (Part III, Keynote Addresses Lele, Touré and Kohn).

The ways in which the evident needs can best be tackled were thoroughly discussed, in particular at the Round Table "Concepts of Research Partnership" (Part III, p. 113). The ways may, or even must, vary from one Northern country to another and from one Southern country or region to another. There was, however, a general consensus on the principle of partnership, which first of all means that one has to get away from the "donor/recipient" mentality. Much emphasis was laid on the value of informal indigenous knowledge, on traditional culture and, therefore, on the willingness to learn from each other (see below, Collected Recommendations).

The potential and the limits of research partnership were discussed by the Panel on International Competition for Research in the South (Part III, p. 119), and most extensively by ten Working Groups (Part III, p. 137). As will be indicated in the General Conclusions, below, the potential of international co-operation in research for development is enormous. But the obstacles to the implementation of equitable research co-operation are considerable. The tendency to look at Northern science as "international" while Southern science is generally considered as merely "local", reflects one of the major hindrances to genuine collaboration, namely the effective dominance of the North.

The dominance of the North was found to affect many aspects of co-operation, from the choice of partners and the planning of research agendas, the management of funds and the access to information, to the possibilities of publishing, the utilization of the results obtained and rights of ownership, to name but some of the difficulties most frequently mentioned. Perhaps, however, the problem that was felt to be worst, was the frequent lack of transparency, ranging from an inadequate definition of the goals of research projects or support actions, down to what can only be termed dishonesty. As one way of avoiding such imbalance, the importance of South-South co-operation was strongly emphasised, although it should not be perceived as a replacement of North-South partnership but rather as a supplement to it. Consequently the North was invited to foster South-South interrelations, to establish South-North-South partnerships and, in general, to contribute to the consolidation of research institutions already existing in the South.

The attitude towards research partnership prevailing in official circles in Switzerland was expressed in the Forum "Swiss Policy in Partnership". Without exception, the speakers recognised research co-operation with developing countries as being of high priority. The representatives of Swiss research institutions expressed the view that Swiss research policy ought to be revised in the light of international collaboration, in particular with developing countries, and that the Swiss National Science Foundation (SNSF) in particular, ought seriously to consider adding the partnership element to the existing criteria of academic value when assessing projects submitted for funding.

The representatives of the Swiss Parliament shared the views of the research institutions, provided that the scientists, on their side, clearly demonstrated the will to adhere to the principles of partnership. They encouraged the Swiss scientific community to provide members of Parliament continuously with accurate information. The Parliamentarians did, however, remind the Swiss scientific community of the serious financial constraints that Switzerland is presently subjected to, and asked them to seek ways of using the financial means available more efficiently.

The views of a representative of the private sector were expressed in the Keynote Address by M. Kohn. He identified ten "braking forces" which could impede collaboration in research between entrepreneurs from the North and researchers in the South. These included pre-conditional constraints, such as the demand for utility, language barriers, financial and stability problems and a lack of infrastructure. Nevertheless, the international scientific community was encouraged to intensify its endeavour to enlist the support of private enterprise.

Examples of scientific collaboration in partnership were presented in a poster exhibition (Annex). A high proportion of the posters shown referred to projects supported by the Priority Programme Environment of the SNSF, a Programme co-financed by SDC and SNSF (see also Part II, last two chapters).

General conclusions

- Together, scientists from all over the world are able and willing to contribute substantially to the knowledge and the tools needed to achieve sustainable global development.
- With reference to development, the goals of scientific research need to be re-defined, at international level and with full participation of the end-users.
- The countries of the South are increasingly aware of their part of the responsibility for improving and maintaining their research capacities.
- The countries in the North are expected to participate in the process as catalysts and partners, in a spirit of unreserved intellectual honesty.
- It is up to the scientific community itself to get the decision-makers, in governments and in the private sector alike, to recognize the potential of research and to give it the support needed.

Collected Recommendations

During the Conference, numerous recommendations were either made explicitly or expressed implicitly both by the speakers on the rostrum and the participants in the discussions. It was felt that a collection of these recommendations, organised under overall headings, would provide an excellent summing-up of the results of the Conference.

The following list is based on notes taken throughout the Conference. Of course, though every effort has been made to take all the recommendations into account, such a summary cannot be exhaustive. For more details, the reader is referred to Part III of the Proceedings, and especially to the first chapter of Part II "Needs and Concepts as seen from the South", and the following section of quotations.

A Recommendations addressed to everyone concerned

A.1 In general terms

- Scientific research with reference to sustainable global development to be redefined[1], without neglecting the human dimension of development[2]
- The right of the community to preserve its culture[3] and to own its collective, traditional knowledge[4] ('informal indigenous knowledge'[5]) to be recognised
- To get away from the donor/recipient attitude[6] and to fight the tendency to consider Northern science 'international' as

---

[1] Messerli, Panel Discussion & Swiss Policy Forum
[2] Castillo
[3] Working Group B
[4] Round Table & Working Group F
[5] Hardie
[6] Swiss Policy Forum

opposed to Southern science thought to be only 'local'[7]
- Partnership to be considered better than aid;[8] the capacities of the partners complementing each other[9]
- Basic sciences and fundamental research to be supported as well as goal-oriented and applied research[10]
- The maintaining of centres of excellence to be supported and the establishment of networks to be encouraged to cater for different geographical regions and research interests[11]
- North-South co-operation to be maintained and even intensified;[12] South-South co-operation, however, as well as 'triangular' North-South-South co-operation, to be strongly emphasised[13]
- 'Open dialogue'[14]: research priorities as well as research agendas - national, regional, international - to be defined by national governments, academia, researchers, donors and end-users[15]
- 'Clear objectives': the goals of each research project to be unmistakably defined;[16] (e.g. capacity-building, human resource development[17], socioeconomic development) and the results evaluated against the set objectives
- End-users to be involved in the process of research-policy making, by donors and the home countries alike[18]
- Dissemination of findings to be rendered possible[19] as a user-oriented knowledge process[20]
- Results to be published in journals accessible to both North

---

[7] Working Group A_2 & Floor
[8] Panel Discussion
[9] Working Group F
[10] Swiss Policy Forum & Floor
[11] Hassan & Working Group G
[12] Hassan
[13] Working Group D
[14] Working Group A_2
[15] Working Groups A_1, F & G
[16] Floor
[17] Working Groups A_{1+2}
[18] Working Groups B & G
[19] Working Group G
[20] Working Groups H & I

and South, as well as in papers accessible to the general public[21]
- Effects of research activities to be evaluated[22]
- Results to get back to the end-users, and protection of intellectual property to be made accessible[23]
- Sustainability to be guaranteed through integration of innovations suggested by local people[24]
- Researchers to defend forcefully the relevance of research priorities and agendas[25]

A.2 In specific terms

- Communication infrastructure to be examined with the objective of making electronic media more accessible and useful to everybody (e.g. e-mail)[26]
- Management of research and development to include Southern partners, with appropriate training where needed[27]
- Budgets to include activities like writing of proposals, writing up results and publishing them (at all levels), and the application for patents[28]
- Incentives for research in partnership to be created[29]
- To exercise great care with reference to the World Bank's Structural Adjustment Programmes[30]

---

[21] Working Groups F, G & H
[22] Working Groups A_{1+2}
[23] Working Group F
[24] Working Group I
[25] Working Groups A_1 & E
[26] Messerli, Working Groups D, F & H
[27] Working Group C & Floor
[28] Working Group F
[29] Working Group C
[30] Working Group B

B Recommendations addressed to countries in the South

B.1 In general terms

- The countries in the South to commit themselves[31] and to establish their own plans of research-policy[32]
- The South to rely on its own resources and to contribute to research for development also financially, e.g. with the help of Regional Foundations[33] (rather than depending too much on unreliable external sources[34])
- Countries in the South to take care of the utilisation of results obtained by research[35] and to be concerned with the participation of the population[36], taking advantage also of national and/or regional NGOs[37]
- The scientific community in the South to get organised, for example by providing directories[38], establishing regional networks of information, training and research[39] including governments[40] (science and the private sector)[41], and training future scientists and researchers to take their places essentially in their own region[42]

---

[31] Round Table
[32] Hassan & Floor
[33] Hassan
[34] Lele
[35] Round Table
[36] Castillo
[37] Khor
[38] Working Group D
[39] Castillo & Working Group D
[40] Swiss Policy Forum & Floor
[41] Panel Discussion
[42] Hassan

B.2 In specific terms
- Governments to guarantee free circulation of scientists and an unhindered flow of scientific information[43]
- Funds to be earmarked for South-South collaboration[44]
- South-South competition for funds from the North to be avoided[45]
- Increase of bureaucracy - "popcorn effect"[46] - connected to research activities to be avoided[47]

C Recommendations addressed to countries in the North
C.1 In general terms
- The North to respect national plans of Southern countries where they exist[48]
- The Northern countries to take the differences between the so-called "developing countries" into consideration and to be constantly aware of the rapid changes occurring in some of them[49]
- The Northern countries to accept long term commitments and to avoid a "stop-and-go" policy[50]
- Northern countries to establish a Code of Conduct for research partnership[51] and to allow free choice of partners by the South[52]
- Transparency of all information to be observed, including funding[53] and salary structures ("intellectual honesty")'[54]

---

[43] Working Group D
[44] Working Group D
[45] Panel Discussion & A_2
[46] Fust
[47] Panel Discussion
[48] Working Groups A_{1+2}
[49] Lele
[50] Floor
[51] Panel Discussion
[52] Castillo & Round Table
[53] Working Groups B & C
[54] Working Group F

- The Northern countries to support higher education in countries of the South[55] as well as existing universities[56] and centres of excellence[57]
- Northern agencies to act as catalysts rather than performers, with special emphasis on multidisciplinarity and gender relations[58]

C.2 In specific terms

- Donors to concern themselves with the support of students after their return[59], and also with re-entry grants for scientists who have worked in another country[60]
- Northern countries to encourage and assist scientists from the South who work abroad ("brain drain") to cooperate with their countries of origin
- Donors to help researchers from the South to prepare research protocols[61]
- Editors of internationally known scientific journals to invite scientists from the South to participate in the work of their Editorial Advisory Boards[62]
- Not only junior but also senior staff from the North to spend adequate time with their partners in the South[63]

---

[55] Round Table
[56] Floor
[57] Hassan
[58] Castillo, Swiss Policy Forum
[59] Working Group F
[60] Working Group E
[61] Working Group E
[62] Floor
[63] Working Group E

Part I	Collected Recommendations

D Recommendations addressed to Switzerland in particular

D.1 In general terms

- The Swiss scientific community to be concerned about open-mindedness and to be prepared to learn from the South[64]
- Swiss research policy to be revised altogether in the light of international co-operation, in particular with developing countries[65] and its revised policy to be made known in the South[66]
- Rules of co-operation to be kept flexible, and collaboration modes, including research partnership at its various levels, to be adapted individually to the conditions of each partner[67]
- A change of mentality of the Swiss scientific community, from an attitude of benevolence to one of true partnership with scholars and scientists from the South, to be brought about[68]
- Members of the Swiss scientific community to clearly demonstrate their will to adhere to the principles of research partnership, to accept evaluation of their work by, among others, partners from the South, to provide politicians and entrepreneurs alike with accurate information and to "lobby" both in view of obtaining the necessary support[69]

---

[64] Schäublin
[65] Swiss Policy Forum
[66] Working Group B
[67] Round Table
[68] Swiss Policy Forum
[69] Swiss Policy Forum & Kohn

D.2 In specific terms

- Swiss National Foundation (SNF) to seriously consider adding the partnership element to the existing criteria of academic value of projects submitted[70]
- SNF to provide financial means for ending research partnership (where ending cannot be avoided) in a decent and respectful manner[71]
- KFPE to revise the *'Swiss Strategy for the Promotion of Scientific Research in Developing Countries'* in view of the goals of research for sustainable development and its applicability in various countries of the 'Third World'[72]
- KFPE to revise its Action Plan, with particular reference to the planned *Information Guide* and the *Guidelines for Research Partnership*[73]
- KFPE to explicitly address the Swiss private sector[74]
- KFPE and SDC to seek ways of more effectively exchanging information among interested countries in the North on collaboration with developing countries[75]
- KFPE and SDC to explore ways of continuing the North-South dialogue on research for sustainable development[76]
- KFPE to explore possibilities of sending young Swiss scientists to universities in the South, of inviting senior scientists from the South as visiting professors to Swiss universities and High Schools, and of making such exchanges easier by working for official scientific exchange agreements among the countries concerned[77]

compiled by Thierry A. Freyvogel & Daniel Maselli

---

[70] Swiss Policy Forum
[71] Högger
[72] Swiss Policy Forum
[73] Freyvogel
[74] Kohn
[75] Panel Discussion
[76] Hassan
[77] Floor

Needs and Concepts as seen from the South

Ana Maria Cetto, Raquel V. Francisco and
Naigzi Gebremedhin. Edited by *Jennifer M. Jenkins,*
based on texts written at the Conference

Partnership in Research for Development

It should be clear that, rather than being synonymous with economic growth, development is to be considered as a sustainable improvement in the quality of human existence. There is a tendency to use only economic indicators, but others may be equally important - like the sustainable use of natural resources, or the affirmation in the development process of issues of social justice.

Any discussion on the contributions of science to development should bear in mind that alongside the improvement of scientific knowledge other changes must take place that are necessary for integral development. It is in this context that we should ask ourselves, "What consequences have the changes brought about by science and technology had for society - both for communities and for their individual members?" The capacity of humanity to innovate technically has grown exponentially, but the capacity to devise effective forms of social innovation lags far behind.

Research in the natural and exact sciences, as they are studied in universities, has become highly specialised and many intellectuals, when confronted with real-life problems, seriously question its relevance. For one thing, informal research and traditional wisdom should also be considered as a valuable part of the knowledge system. In re-thinking international scientific cooperation, this informal component of the knowledge system - which in poorer countries is normally stronger than the formal one - should be seriously taken into account.

The most urgent national concerns in most countries in the South are the alleviation of poverty, and socio-economic development. Research is needed to improve production and to ensure that resources are managed in a sustainable way. The carrying out of this research needs local scientists, who will be better able to take into consideration the traditional and informal knowledge that already exists, and to understand the social system and the way people interact with each other and with the environment, than people coming from another country and another culture. However, in many countries in the South there is not yet sufficient research capacity to do the work that is urgently required.

The building of research capacity in countries of the South is vital, but it will inevitably be a long-term process. Partnership between North and South will be needed for many years to come. The present chapter discusses the need to strengthen research capacity and research institutions in the South, and the way in which research partnerships can contribute to solving not only the specific problems posed by development in the South, but also the global problems that are of common concern to everyone.

The need to strengthen research capacity in the South

It is vital for countries in the South to have a competent local scientific community to address both local and global concerns. A scientific community that commands respect can influence the policies of governments and the setting of research agendas. Scientists can help to convince policy-makers and the public of the need to address global concerns, like the problems of the environment, and explain their implications and their possible impact in the future. Furthermore, if governments involved in negotiations can draw on the support of well-informed local opinion, they will be better able to prevent research agendas being dominated by industrialised countries. This can happen not only in global programmes, but in local and national programmes that are funded from the North. Funding agencies, whether governments, international

Part II   Needs and Concepts as seen from the South

organisations, NGOs or the private sector, will have their own priorities and concerns, and may not always respect the national research policies or the local needs of the Southern partner. Donors often favour some kinds of projects over others - for example a research centre in India reported that in the 1980s it was hard to obtain money for environmental projects, but in the 1990s these are almost the only projects that are funded.

The knowledge gap between North and South is already wide, and is becoming wider as a result of the rapid development of science and technology in the North. Research capacity is not easy to assess, either qualitatively or quantitatively, and there is a need to develop more refined ways of measuring it. However, there are some relevant statistics; for example that 80% of the world's people live in the South, but they include only 24% of the world's scientists and engineers, and of these, only a small percentage are actually engaged in research and development. Even when one remembers that the figures do not include "informal research" - the process of observation and learning by experience that has given rise to a large body of traditional knowledge - these numbers clearly indicate an imbalance. There are, of course, big differences within the South. Countries like India, Brazil, Argentina and China have higher research capacities and account for 6% of the 8% of research funds allocated in developing countries. A broad belt around the equator is virtually ignored, and countries which are unstable politically often find it difficult to obtain funding.

Why are the numbers of people engaged in research in the South so low? One concern expressed at the conference was that the quality of education is deteriorating, and without a firm basis in education it is impossible to develop a body of competent scientists. Student numbers are rising, but there has been no proportionate increase in facilities. The role that could be played by universities in furthering development is not always appreciated by governments, which may indeed suspect them of fomenting political opposition. Those working in universities often feel that there is a tendency to forget that basic science is needed as a foundation for any kind of scientific activity, and there is a failure to appreciate the importance of basic research. On the other hand, universities do need to see themselves as part of the economic process, and be prepared not only to carry out applied research on problems of national concern, but to communicate their results to the public. Scientists working in universities and other institutions could contribute a great deal to building research capacity, but the fact that research workers are so often evaluated purely on the basis of publications does not encourage them to devote time and energy to training others.

Another problem is that in the South, research as a profession is often not attractive, because of lack of resources and the weakness of research institutions. Many well-qualified people find it so difficult to work in their own countries that they decide to go elsewhere. However, one speaker reminded the conference participants that this "brain-drain" should not be seen as entirely negative. It might be better to talk about the "brain circulation" which results from mobility. This can be a positive resource. However, a certain "critical mass" does have to be reached before research can function effectively. One way in which this might be achieved is by the concentration of efforts on particular topics in centres of excellence which could be regional rather than national.

There is also wastage because the qualified people who do remain in their own countries do not have the resources they need to use their abilities to the full. There is a need for the building of capacity for the management of research programmes and institutions. Another aspect of wastage is that because of the limited information highway from North to South, or South to South, publications and reports of work done earlier are often not available, so it is difficult to build on what has been done before.

It is clear that if global problems are to be solved, there needs to be more research capacity in the South. However, in a world where cooperation is vital, the capacity of the North to understand the situation in the South must also be maintained and increased. The era when large numbers of scientists from the North spent their working lives in research projects in the South is long past, because there are plenty of qualified local researchers. But it is important that people from the North should still have opportunities not just to visit countries in the South briefly, but really to live and work there for a sustained period. That is a prerequisite for real understanding, without which there can be no fruitful partnership.

The Concept of Research Partnership

First and foremost, research partnership should always be looked at as an intercultural dialogue and an intellectual relationship, not as a mere transfer of knowledge or funds. Methods developed in such an exchange should always be based on mutual trust and principles of reciprocity, responsibility, equity and transparency, and should represent a gain for both sides, so as to guarantee their sustainability and long-lasting effects. Finally, one should bear in mind that research partnerships not only produce research; among other things they also produce human relations and long-term alliances.

Capacity-building is a vital objective of research partnership. It is important to include this aspect specifically in the planning of research projects, and in evaluating research it is necessary to examine the results not only in terms of the papers and reports produced, but even more importantly in terms of the capacity-building achieved. The budgets for projects should include a capacity-building component, so that something will be left behind when the project is over. Experience has shown that it is easier to build capacity than to maintain and use it. Regional cooperation, with the establishment of thematic networks, can help to maintain capacities, make full use of them and develop them further. Donors who want to support local institutions need to do this in a sustained way over a long term, in some cases for 15-20 years.

The goals and agendas of research partnership

An obvious arena for research partnership is the environment and global changes. Awareness of the global effects of our actions became manifest in 1992 in Rio, where long-term commitments were subscribed to by the governments of North and South. Nevertheless, the agenda of global investigations, like many others, is still dominated by the North, and there is an urgent need to change this situation. However, in this as in other aspects a basic question remains: how can the South make rapid changes without losing its equilibrium? The only way to address this question is by carrying out research on development issues, and by extending North-South contacts so as to get a better understanding of the problems, conditions and potentialities of developing countries.

In all cases, in defining the research agenda both sides must have clear goals, and state clearly what they are aiming at. Partnership projects should be really multidisciplinary, so as to ensure that the social aspects are properly addressed. Small, holistic projects may be more effective than large projects that look at phenomena in isolation.

The agenda is also vulnerable to political considerations. There is considerable pressure to address and focus on immediate issues rather than basic research. This is illustrated by the situation in agriculture, where the International Service for National Agricultural Research (ISNAR) now emphasises testing and demonstration as opposed to basic research. Some speakers at the conference were unhappy about this emphasis on practical problems, and felt that research partnership should not evolve into a crude utilitarian programme. Others considered that research should address immediate issues and the aspirations of the end-users, such as the alleviation of poverty and the provision of simple and cost-effective solutions for problems of day to day life, and stressed the need to establish a research agenda that is demand driven. However, it was also pointed out that if development-oriented research gets the reputation of being low quality research, it is doomed to failure.

Research partnership in practice

The right choice of partners is important. They should be chosen according to the skills and experience each can offer. In defining partnership projects, the widely different conditions from one developing country to the other, and even within countries, must be borne in mind. It is hardly realistic to expect equality in all respects, but there should always be equivalence of partners, and an equitable relationship in as many aspects as possible, including gender. Partnership on a level of intellectual equality requires equal access to means of information. This calls for an information policy, as a joint responsibility of politicians, decision-makers and scientists. Electronic media, CD-ROM and Internet in particular, can become useful tools, but the cost may make them inaccessible to scientists in many countries.

Many current research projects involve partnerships between universities or established research centres. These institutions have the advantage of a long tradition and relative stability. However, research projects can involve a wide variety of partners. For example, many NGOs now perceive that research can be a necessary instrument to bring about changes in the economic and social system. This brings new challenges for research partnership, for example as a result of the demanding tasks associated with complex negotiations in the world trade, and the proliferation of complex legal provisions for ensuring bio-safety and protecting the environment. NGOs may be particularly well placed to tackle some of these. There should also be opportunities to increase collaboration in research between the public sector and the private sector, especially when dealing with research topics in which immediate practical application is an important feature. Although in many countries in the South the proportion of the economy controlled by the private sector is already large, or is rapidly increasing , this sector does not carry out or support much research. Corporate funding tends to be limited to the direct interests of the multinational corporation providing the money. It is, of course, also true of other donors that the kinds of projects funded will reflect their current interests. One example given was that in the energy sector grants are more readily available for environment-related issues than for policy-related ones.

Clearly, research programmes will inevitably be affected by the political climate in all the countries involved. Research cannot thrive in a country where the government is not convinced of its value. Donors are also affected by political considerations, and they tend to crowd into politically stable countries, preferably those with a healthy climate for guest research workers. There is also the danger that competition within or between countries for projects and funds will lead to influence-buying, which can compromise the ethical basis of research projects severely.

The use and dissemination of the results

The issues of transfer, dissemination, use and implementation of the results of research projects are of much concern. Colleagues from developing countries often claim that the results of research partnership are not always used locally, and it is a fact that often this research is geared towards the interests of private companies and multinational corporations. The problem of the ownership of the products of research has become more acute recently - as a result of international trade agreements, knowledge has increasingly become a commodity. It is therefore recommended that transfer to the end user, and implementation of the results, should be an integral part of project planning from the outset.

Scientific journals have an important role to play both in the dissemination of research results and in promoting further research. Journals produced in the North are an important means of international communication, and it is recommended that they should include colleagues from the South in their refereeing and editorial bodies. Means should also be found to make publications from the South better known and more readily available everywhere. However, there is also an important place for publications designed for a readership in a particular region, addressing questions of local importance, and these should also be supported.

Different models of partnership

The speakers at the Conference, and those who contributed posters, gave many examples of research projects large and small being carried out on a basis of partnership. Representatives of several governments and institutions illustrated the variety of possible models. In Sweden, where university education is closely linked to research, capacity building through education is an essential element of research partnership, and the university establishment is regarded as the heart or venue of research. The speaker from the Netherlands pointed out that a key concept of partnership is empowerment, and this needs long-term financial support, for 10-15 years. The asymmetry between North and South cannot simply be ignored, but the effects can be counteracted by ensuring that decision-making bodies include the Southern partners - even when those bodies are located in the North - and by ensuring that the setting of the research agenda is a genuine consultative process in which all partners have a voice.

Another way in which the influence of single donors can be decreased is by strengthening international institutions such as the UN, and by including a number of partners from North and South in multilateral projects. It is clear that research partnership does not only involve North-South links. There are already projects in many regions involving cooperation between Southern partners. This is an area of cooperation with considerable potential for growth.

Finally, however, it must be emphasised that international cooperation can never be a substitute for national development plans; strengthening national research systems is the only viable recourse for a stable and sustained development. Domination by donor countries or organisations is inevitable when weak national research structures exist, and donors step into a virtual vacuum. There is a need to strengthen or establish national institutions such as research councils, which can, for example, create information systems to find out what is being done by whom, and formulate and enforce codes of ethical conduct for research.

Selected Statements of Representatives of the South

"The question of who defines research agendas in the South depends upon funding situations, the influence of global ideas on national research communities, and the knowledge base, technical competence and motivation of Southern researchers. Radically reduced local funding possibilities have meant that Southern researchers now heavily rely on Northern sources of funding. In most cases, these funds are driven by the big issues or ideas that are produced in the North for global consumption (...) It is not that these issues do not have local or national relevance in the South. They do. However, there are two main problems with such types of externally-driven agendas. First, Southern researchers sometimes tend to engage these issues largely from the perspectives of those who first defined them as important - posing the same questions, quoting the same authors, and using the same methodology and analytical categories even when local realities demand a search for new categories and new questions. Second, reliance on globally-produced research agendas often prevents national researchers and their foreign collaborators from working on issues that do not quite fit the global fads, even though such issues might be very relevant for understanding and assisting local and national development."

Yusuf Bangura
United Nations Research Institute for Social Development, Geneva
Initiator of the Working Group on
Research Agendas

Part II Selected Statements of Representatives of the South

„ Nowadays, in the context of pursuit of the knowledge that is growing in the North, scientists from the South are always playing 'catch up' to collect information from the North, and constantly battle to transfer their findings to the North. This has led to a lack of international scientific coverage of discoveries or important scientific findings between North and South and South and South. The interest of both parties in transfers of findings is hampered by whether findings are dealing with narrow or broadly focused fields of research and many other aspects."

Lotfia El Nadi
Universities of Cairo and Qatar
Initiator of the Working Group on
Transfer of Findings

„ Any discussion of the current constraints on research partnership needs an overview of the institutional framework within which research is carried out in the South. More specifically, it requires a close look at the research capability in terms of setting up a research agenda, prioritising the same to meet the needs of the society, the ability to transform goals into research plans, and incorporating research initiatives originating from the North in such a perspective. (...) The research and development environment in the South has a dampening effect on the ability of the researchers in the South to shape a proper research agenda and in that process to negotiate research partnerships on an equal basis with funding agencies, and research institutions from the North. Very often, the collaborations of the North-South research partnerships take place with personal contacts. Research grants by and large are received by the best researchers and the best institutions and, therefore, have little effect on capacity building."

K.N. Nair
Centre for Development Studies, Kerala, India
Initiator of the Working Group on
Constraints on Research Partnerships

„One of the fundamental reasons that explains the slow advance of scientific development in Third World countries is the lack of perception of our societies about the importance of endogenous science for the cultural and socioeconomic development of our countries. Lack of priority rather than lack of funds is our main problem. This situation is difficult to reverse since it requires us to educate our political and financial leaders and the whole of society itself. Developing country scientists must learn how to build bridges to connect with their societies if they are to achieve support for their projects and their ideas. This activity of scientific lobbying is needed in all the developing countries."

Jorge E. Allende
Network on Biological Sciences, University of Chile
Initiator of the Working Group on
South-South Scientific Collaboration

„The project should fit into the *local organisation structure* at the micro-level, and deal with a complete set of limiting factors, i.e. all the basic constraints to the local development. The research process requires a group decision on the field survey: the scientists, the representatives of the local authorities, and the inhabitants join in the project planning to make sure that the contexts of different research activities are aimed at the hopes of all the partners (about the improvement of the environment and the living conditions of the selected sites). This procedure enforces *practices of local decision making*, and *interdisciplinary research* right in the first activities of the project. For long range planning, the projects should enrol trainees for the basic education/ training in appropriate disciplines as well as in interdisciplinary practices."

Bui thi Lang
Dept. of Science, Technology and Environment, Ho Chi Minh City, Vietnam
Initiator of the Working Group on
Access to Knowledge and Results

Part II Selected Statements of Representatives of the South

„ Beyond material rewards, whether in a narrow or in a broader sense, some other kinds of rewards may be considered as non-material: for instance, self-satisfaction and esteem for one's own contribution to the progress of knowledge. (...) In this respect, it must be clear that scientists and other academics in the South suffer not only from low salaries and material poverty, but also, sometimes, from the underestimation of their activity by their governments and populations. Therefore, not only is intellectual labour underpaid, as are most forms of honest labour, but, what is worse, it does not provide, at least in some countries in the South, the social consideration and esteem one should have expected. (...) To that extent at least, inequity is as much a domestic problem as an international one; the necessary changes must come from the inside. "

Paulin J. Hountondji
University of Benin; Former Minister
Initiator of the Working Group on
Equity in Reward Systems

statements compiled by Beat Sottas

Part II

It was evident at the conference, and will be evident to readers of these Proceedings, that there was a very large area of agreement between contributors from the North and the South about what needs to be done. There was also a strong feeling that it is time to translate this unity of purpose into concrete actions - and that such actions will only be fruitful in terms of scientific partnership if they are carried out in a spirit of complete openness and intellectual honesty.

The next chapter discusses what "a new agenda for partnership" might look like. It has been written since the conference, and it represents a view from the North, since all members of the drafting team were from Switzerland. The chapter can thus be compared to the previous one, "Needs and Concepts as seen from the South", which was written during the last day of the conference by a group of experts from the South who were members of the drafting committee for the executive summary.

The editors

Towards a Shift in Research for Development
A new Agenda for Partnership

Jacques Forster and *Beat Sottas*

Preamble

The present chapter was drafted by a team based in Switzerland, led by Prof. **Jacques Forster** from the Graduate Institute of Development Studies in Geneva (IUED). The members accepted the challenge: (i) to assess experiences gained in research collaboration, (ii) to reconsider the case for partnership, and (iii) to outline the rationale for a shift in the partnership agenda. The following contributed to the chapter: Prof. **Marcel Tanner** from the Swiss Tropical Institute, Dr. **Peter Trutmann**, Executive Manager of the Centre for International Agriculture based at the Swiss Federal Institute of Technology, Mr. **Adrian Hadorn**, Head of the Policy and Research Section of the Swiss Agency for Development and Cooperation (SDC), Dr. **Urs Herren**, Research Policy Desk in SDC's Policy and Research Section, and Dr. **Beat Sottas**, Executive Secretary of the Conference, who compiled and edited the paper.

The various contributions discussed at the Conference addressed a broad spectrum of questions. This review aims at synthesising key issues, mainly by focusing on the conceptual and strategic levels of research partnership. It embraces three different parts: 1) an overview of past paradigms and current trends, 2) an evaluation of the Conference, and, 3) an outline of elements for a new agenda for partnership.

Although based on the deliberations of the Conference, these considerations reflect a view from the North because there was no representative from the South involved in the drafting. However, since the previous article presents an assessment made by experts from the South, we are confident that the readers will find it stimulating to compare the two analyses.

1. Overview

1.1. Trends and approaches in the past

For many decades, large amounts of money - raised by international agencies, universities, NGOs, industry and other sources - have been spent on funding a broad variety of research, including collaborative efforts with developing countries. The prominent feature of all these attempts is that research was conducted by individuals or small groups and in a few instances by networks. Consequently, there was - and still is - a confusing array of research initiatives in the North directed at problems in the South. There is, to some extent, like-mindedness regarding the necessity of supporting research in the South, but the lack of co-ordination and guiding principles leads to situations where research partners in the South may be approached by different sponsors at the same time. Experience also shows that research collaboration is in most cases offer-driven; subsequently, this leads to a domination by those who have raised and/or hold the funds.

Among developing countries contrasting attitudes towards research prevail. Whereas some countries grant research a high priority, a lack of coherent and clear national research plans is characteristic in many cases. This state of affairs has adverse effects at different levels: (i) at the highest level it limits the emergence of coherent national policies and limits their potential, (ii) at an intermediate level it prevents organisations and institutions from building capacity, and finding appropriate forms of cooperation, and (iii) at the lowest level it prevents individual researchers from establishing committed relationships.

In parallel with political, economic and cultural globalisation and the inherent predominance of the North, there is an international division of labour regarding scientific development. The world system of knowledge production and management seems to reserve to the North the monopoly of conceptualisation and invention, whereas the South is expected to supply data as well as to apply results and inventions. Northern researchers appear to be powerful because they deal with theoretical and conceptual issues; Southern partners - often seen as junior associates - implement research and collect data.

Although the situation varies considerably from one region of the world to another, in many countries the state of teaching and research institutions has been deteriorating continuously over the last years, and the brain drain has increased. At present, financial constraints occurring as an effect of the prevailing austerity policies threaten the achievements of the 1970s and 1980s, endangering the capacity gained and the structures that have been established. As a result, many institutions continue to depend on foreign support. Their acute need, combined with this dependence, puts them in a very weak and exposed position, and they are rarely able to develop demand-driven agendas. Consequently, unequal power and capacities favour top-down decision-making dictated by external actors. This state is reinforced by a growing dominance of global themes. Since large donor organisations operate as trend-setters, they limit the scope for influence by national research agencies and they also force researchers to adapt to global research trends.

For many researchers, reaching an international audience is often the first priority, and is far more important than capacity or institution building, relevance and applicability. Researchers from the South often blame colleagues from the North for pursuing their own careers. They feel they are victims of a "data-for-donations" attitude where they are instrumentalised and exploited, sometimes simply to allow the Northern partner to bypass procedures linked to research clearances or customs regulations. Moreover, there is another important issue when assessing research activities in the South. It may occur that key position holders become researchers not necessarily through choice but through processes of patronage, administrative procedures and careers as functionaries. Thus they often lack motivation and have no genuine interest in scientific topics, and also no awareness of the potential of scientific networking.

In general, one may summarise that research collaboration has a backlog in both the underlying concepts and in practice in comparison to the mainstream of development cooperation. In this domain, important shifts regarding the approach have occurred since the 1950s. Initially, development cooperation focused on technical solutions and infrastructural development; in the 1970s cooperation addressed human resources development, and finally, in the mid-eighties, the need arose to focus on partnership, and as a result sophisticated participatory methodologies were developed. Moreover, new approaches aimed at addressing the framing conditions and enhancing a policy dialogue. In the domain of research, concepts of partnership did not develop at the same pace. Research was quite protected from exposure to emerging trends in development cooperation, as well as from changes in the expectations and needs of developing countries. Accordingly, the necessity jointly to formulate aims and goals of research - the agenda in the strict sense - is a rather recent phenomenon. Attempts are now being made, but there are still deficits in research policies at both programme and project levels. What is still lacking is first of all the political will to create a favourable policy framework and, in a second step, the elaboration of methodologies for joint agenda setting at national level, as well as methodologies focusing on a dialogue addressing the policy framework at national and programme levels.

1.2. Towards a new style in scientific collaboration

This somewhat pessimistic assessment is due, among other factors, to the fact that up to now the concept of partnership in research for development has not yet been fully elaborated. In development cooperation, participation in and ownership of projects by partners from the South have become key principles. This must also apply to scientific capacity building. In order to reach this goal, a combination of components located at different levels is necessary to constitute a local *research system*: qualified people (human resources), an adequate organisational and institutional base for the research community, and finally an enabling national environment which supports and sustains research activities. Research partnerships which take into account all these facets would allow relevant issues to be identified, matters of common concern to be effectively tackled, and the responsibilities for a sustainable development to be shared. Such joint efforts are needed to find appropriate responses to the increasingly complex and heterogeneous issues which affect our common future.

There are indeed many good reasons for advocating a partnership approach in research for development. Given the fact that an undeniable institutional adjustment is taking place in the higher education sector and the research organisations of the North, academic teaching and research have to address new themes evolving from common concerns at global level and based on local priorities. This requires a significant strengthening of human capacities in the North and South, as this is a prerequisite for an exchange between partners who are different but have common concerns. The North has to invest enough in order to assure capacity building at all levels because this will facilitate the mutuality of interests and benefits.

Aside from personal commitments deriving from research partnership, the following arguments show the need for and the potential benefits of a reorientation.
- First of all, collaborative efforts facilitate and strengthen the gaining of insights; they should increase the relevance and site specificity of research projects.
- Second, the evolving synergisms always constitute a comparative advantage; they should lead to more professionalism and effectiveness in dealing with priority questions and issues.
- Third, awareness should create a like-mindedness which fosters the sharing of responsibilities.

An approach following the concepts of research consortia, networks of collaborators and triangular relationships could serve as a model. Due to their multilateral character, these forms avoid the pitfalls that occur in bilateral or bipolar arrangements between researchers and organisations. A *con-*

sortium has comparative advantages, because it is formally organised among a limited number of institutions which agree on a common research agenda with clearly defined areas of responsibility, division of labour and the sharing of resources. *Networks* are more informal with a broad participation by persons and organisations interested in a specific topic. However, they often take time before they really lead to synergism. *Triangular relationships* between an industrialised country, an advanced developing country and a less developed country may be implemented with the aim of achieving a good equilibrium and buffering predominances. Thus, centres of excellence in countries such as India, South Africa, Brazil and Thailand may become mediators. Up to now, relatively little experience has been gained with this form. It is assumed that there is a fair chance for positive effects, although centre-periphery conflicts and tendencies towards regional hegemony may remain.

At present, advanced communication technologies are often praised for their potential for providing world-wide access to knowledge and to scientific audiences. It is believed that they could empower researchers in the South, because scientists working in widely-dispersed places can be in close touch with one another, and can use effective networks as virtual research institutions. While we agree that these innovations can facilitate conceptual changes and foster partnerships, we would also like to stress that prevailing structural dependencies cannot be made to disappear by modern exchange media. In this context, it is important to consider also the critical voices that note that these new tools in communication might not solve the problems related to intercultural dialogue and that they do not necessarily lead to a more equitable distribution of scientific competence. On the contrary, it is pointed out that they could favour a concentration of information and knowledge in the scientific centres in the North. This, in turn, might hamper the establishment of a joint responsibility for common concerns.

Part II — Towards a Shift in Research for Development

A new style in research collaboration has already been introduced in various fields; the CGIAR system and the UNDP/World Bank/WHO Special Programme for Research and Training in Tropical Diseases might be mentioned as prominent examples.

The UNDP/World Bank/WHO Special Programme for Research and Training in Tropical Diseases created networks by applying two strategies:

1. The initiation of large multi-site studies, by taking one subject and addressing it in different endemic settings. This approach not only requires links between teams from North and South but also interdisciplinary teams constituted by biomedical and social scientists for each site.

These networks formed the basis for further research and also significantly facilitated the crossing of barriers between e.g. research institutions and ministries. Moreover, it facilitated the transfer of research results to applications.

2. The implementation of regional small grants programmes in South America and Africa created networks between social scientists and biomedical researchers of the region.

These topic-oriented teams were linked by locally/regionally administered research grants, but their links with the North were not related to research funding procedures.

The CGIAR system is an informal association of 48 public and private sector members, including members from the South, that supports a network of 16 international agricultural research centres. The CGIAR conducts strategic and applied research to promote sustainable agriculture, and focuses on interdisciplinary programs implemented by one or more of its international centres together with a full range of partners.

The CGIAR uses regional and international networks as well as consortia to operationalise research partnerships. The prevailing donor-recipient relationships must give way to equal working partnerships, particularly needed and furthered at five levels:
- between different National Agricultural Research Centres;
- between National Agricultural Research Centres and International Agricultural Research Centres;
- within National Research Centres;
- with Extension Services and Farmers;
- with Centres of Excellence.

Moreover, regional and national centres are considered in the agenda-setting, and the strong centres promote the weak centres.

2. Evaluation of the Conference

In retrospect, we must first acknowledge the very positive climate created by the Conference. However, in view of addressing what remains to be done for the drawing up of a new partnership agenda in research for development we would like to reflect on some of the achievements and on tasks for the future.

2.1. The achievements

The Conference was an important milestone. It allowed the issue of partnership to be addressed for the first time within the Swiss scientific community. Thanks to an important contribution (with respect to both quantity and quality) of colleagues from the South, the Conference succeeded in raising awareness of the partnership issue in a broad range of academic institutions, research organisations and research funding agencies both in Switzerland and abroad. It offered an opportunity to learn from the pitfalls and restrictions encountered in the past, as well as experiences gained in various contexts, and offered a forum for expressing views and discussing innovative concepts and non-discriminating strategies.

The Conference has shown that there is a common understanding and shared conviction about the necessity of North-South as well as South-South partnerships. Differentiated statements based on a variety of experiences demonstrated that a common understanding of prevailing or emerging difficulties is developing. Capacity-building is seen as the core of all attempts at improving partnership. However, it is recognised that this is not a unilateral duty of the sponsors, because all parties involved have to provide significant inputs on the operational level, as well as on the policy level where a dialogue addressing the policy framework has to take place. The goals embrace both research and development, but it is asserted that basic research constitutes the essential part. With respect to the development of capacities, it is important to emphasise that a significant potential can only develop on a basis that ensures a critical mass, i.e. by the consolidation of a research system as outlined above.

The exposure at the Conference to more established and more sophisticated concepts of partnership in research for development, as formulated for example in the Netherlands, Sweden or Canada, was an enriching and very stimulating experience for many research policy makers.

One of the most remarkable results is the triggering of a clear awareness in the political arena and among political decision-makers in Switzerland. With the introduction of new concepts based on principles already implemented in the domain of development cooperation, it is expected that the Conference will have an impact on decision-making, for example in Parliament and in the research funding agencies, in promoting appropriate principles and new strategies for funding research in developing countries.

2.2. What remains to be done

The Conference was a first attempt to address issues related to research partnership. The following is a contribution to the definition of a future agenda.

- The most prominent untouched domain is a definition of the concept of "partnership", which still allows many interpretations. Given the like-mindedness and the many affirmative presuppositions prevailing, many issues are - unfortunately - assumed to have been clarified already.
- At this initial stage, the Conference could not come up with options for an operationalisation of the various approaches for achieving effective research partnerships.
- Imbalances and unequal partnerships are distinct from personal issues; like-mindedness and goodwill may facilitate equity in face-to-face exchanges, but structural constraints and discriminations also have to be addressed - and overcome.
- Research for development has to address adequately regional disparities, priorities and biases. Attention is to be paid to phenomena of domination and mutual ignorance

between advanced developing countries and less developed countries.
- Capacity-building represents a challenge to the higher education sector. Moreover, it has to be accompanied by an adequate reward system which creates proper incentives to encourage intellectuals and knowledge producers. However, the needed increase of salaries and the costs for infrastructure for teaching and research are not affordable for many countries. Accordingly, priority has to be given to quality and critical mass, and not to having many superficially trained people.
- Governments and national institutions put great emphasis on universities; often a strong belief in, and pride in national universities is predominant. In many cases, this attitude is indirectly confirmed by donors, who support existing structures. However, in view of the fact that universities increasingly lack sound competencies and resources for teaching, their role as adequately qualified partners needs to be reconsidered. In this respect, partners in universities are only one option among other actors.
- The exclusive focus on national universities may hamper the sharing of costs through multinational collaboration in the higher education sector. Regional cooperation in teaching has the potential to alleviate the deteriorating situation at the national level.
- It is becoming increasingly important to combine the capacities and competencies of natural or "hard" sciences and social sciences. The prevailing multi-disciplinary patchwork constitutes only the first stage of a comprehensive interdisciplinary approach and a transdisciplinary understanding. Thus, emphasis has to be laid on the building of bridges and forms of dialogue which will lead to the best possible synergism.
- Science and technology are showing a shift towards privatisation, resulting in a higher dependency on the interests of private companies and multinational corporations. Knowledge has also become a commodity linked to particular property rights (this is, for example, well reflected in the

area of biodiversity). This tendency is strengthened by the TRIPS regulations of the WTO.

3. A shift towards more effective partnership approaches

3.1. The case for more partnership in research for development

With a view to achieving sustainable development in both North and South, Agenda 21, accepted at the Rio Summit, outlines the path to be followed. Though it must be noted that some representatives from the South consider it to be one-sided, this action plan does indicate what kind of homework has to be done by research policy makers, funding organisations and researchers themselves in order to reach sustainability in the 21st century. Reaching this goal requires a departure from offer-driven research collaboration and from residual paternalism. Balanced partnerships and common agenda-setting are of crucial importance. All attempts have to start where the Southern partners are and not where the North wants (or expects) them to be. However, a shift in the agenda setting is an issue which does not only concern the North.

A fundamental change of prevailing attitudes is also needed in the South: governments have to set priorities at the policy level and to create appropriate frameworks which allow for the development of a self-confident research system. This, in turn, will increase the bargaining power of researchers from the South and can facilitate the elaboration of a joint agenda. It appears that this is the only way to tackle common concerns from both ends and to assure that responsibility is shared. Research for development has to address regional disparities, priorities and biases adequately. Moreover, as mentioned before, attention has to be paid to phenomena of domination occurring between partners.

Prevailing concepts of research constitute another sensitive issue. The predominant Western scientific knowledge is fragmented, and the approaches tend to be based on reductionist methodologies. Increasing specialisation leads to a loss of holistic and comprehensive understanding. As a consequence of the predominance of Northern preferences and concepts, stakeholders in North and South have different expectations and often operate on the basis of different premises. Experience has shown that these circumstances adversely affect research collaboration.

In such a setting, new methodological orientations are needed. In order to reduce the disparities between North and South, between the more developed and the less developed South as well as between different categories of stakeholders, like-minded partners can effectively play the role of mediators and address both national priorities and field realities. The joint identification of an issue as a common concern may lead to an appreciation of the value of indigenous, local knowledge, which is often underestimated. This issue also raises the question of the selection of partners. Given the fact that insights relevant to end-users and societal concerns are very often gained by actors outside the narrowly defined "scientific community", a more appropriate approach will be to broaden the spectrum of potential partners and take into consideration also the potentials and priorities of local NGOs and associations.

One of the most crucial prerequisites for a change of the prevailing attitudes is a shift in the agenda-setting of research funding agencies. Since they are key players, their currently low awareness of common concerns, as well as the lack of a commitment to share benefits and responsibilities, is inappropriate. A consciencisation - stimulated and facilitated by examples of effective partnerships - has to lead to a reorientation of North-South research policies. Besides a distinct scientific rationale in terms of synergism, on a purely pragmatic level partnerships allow for a more efficient allocation of resources. Collaborative efforts, therefore, can also offer a promising and sound compensation for declining research funds. Once networks and consortia have been established and are operating effectively, they considerably reduce transaction costs: time for designing proposals, negotiating and consolidating institutional arrangements and responsibilities, mobilising funds and dealing with authorities that provide clearances. The resources needed for the building of capacity among research teams can also be reduced.

Research partnerships also have to consider the status of intellectuals in the wider political context. In many developing countries, there is little esteem for the researchers' contribution to the progress of development of the country; some even suffer from political harassment. Therefore, measures of empowerment have to accompany the construction of partnerships, mainly by backing existing research communities vis-à-vis their own local and national governments.

3.2. Principles for balanced partnerships

The authors of the present article are aware that principles for partnership are difficult to make operational in many of the given contexts. Consequently, there are no "blanket solutions" for achieving effective partnerships. Basically, the normative aspects and concepts are much easier to handle than any change in the institutionalised patterns which derive from a long tradition of interaction between dissimilar actors with unequal responsibility, power, capacities, and means. Considering this situation, partnerships constitute an innovative approach to further research for development. The interaction between actors and interests as well as providers and beneficiaries facilitates the identification and tackling of relevant issues.

This section, which aims at outlining the key principles, consists of three parts. In a first step, the new concepts and approaches are summarised, the second part lists elements of a code of conduct, and the third part refers to the challenges for the different actors.

Elements outlined in previous sections showed some prerequisites and starting points. In order to achieve this *shift*

towards innovative approaches for effective partnership, the following aspects need consideration:
- Given the fact that the South includes regions with varying degrees of development, research partnerships have to operate at the appropriate level and to find the most effective form according to the existing frameworks and capacities.
- Research partnerships should evolve from an intercultural dialogue. Besides the intellectual exchange, adequate communication in the literal and technical sense is a prerequisite.
- Although this might facilitate fund-raising, promising research should not primarily follow topics which evolve from current trends in the development debate or the scientific community in general. The research agenda should rather emanate from the topics and methodologies which constitute the mainstream in research for development, or from the actor categories concerned, such as the end-users, local associations, and NGOs.
- A reorientation has also to consider the change of socio-political climate. The tendency towards privatisation leads to a new division of tasks and the emergence of potential new actors: NGOs, associations, consultancy firms and resource centres can also offer relevant contributions to issues of common concern and priority.

In order successfully to achieve a reorientation, the authors propose the following elements of a possible ***code of conduct*** for individual researchers and research institutions:
- Research partnerships should address ethical questions first. The protection of the weaker partner and the mutuality of interests and benefits should precede organisational measures which could lead to more efficiency and higher returns.
- Research partnerships should be balanced. Equity, and thus inclusiveness on an equal footing, are crucial and must be based on like-mindedness, mutual trust, reciprocity and transparency. They should aim at reducing asymmetric

relationships and at keeping a balanced bargaining power as well as an equitable, agreed weight in decision-making.
- In research for development, the selection of the topic should be demand-oriented and represent a local or national priority.
- Research partnerships should clarify the assumptions, expectations and claims to ownership of each partner. This helps to avoid hidden agendas or vested interests. Moreover, it reduces the room for protectionism regarding particular interests on either side in general, and regarding the North's interests in particular. Proper clarification beforehand should help to prevent the kind of research partnership where the collaboration ends up as a data-exporting enterprise with minimal building of research capacity.
- Research partnerships should be based on complementarity through the combination of existing human capital, economic assets, scientific competencies and access to platforms and networks. The joint venture enhances a concentration of scientific and management capacities.
- Research partnerships should assure incentives and an adequate reward system; moreover, they should enhance the reputation of the disciplines and of all parties involved.
- As for the benefits in general, it should be assured that results gained in equal partnerships fit into local priorities and reach the end-users.
- The sharing of responsibilities and common concerns should imply a joint, fair evaluation of results, progress, impacts and benefits.

The above mentioned principles constitute **challenges for different actors**:
- *Researchers* maintain and strengthen their interest in tackling demand-driven research by applying conventional and novel approaches and by linking more closely with peers and research beneficiaries. This implies that both sides need to be sensitised to, and trained in, concepts and methodologies for achieving partnership.

- *People responsible for research programmes, and donors,* have to be aware that capacity- and institution-building are not automatic side-effects of research collaboration. Two key issues have to be tackled: (i) the elaboration of methodologies for joint agenda setting and (ii) the elaboration of approaches which facilitate the combination of scientific excellence and capacity-building; in order to achieve those two different goals, appropriate instruments have to be created and implemented.
- *Donors and research funding agencies* in North and South also contribute to research for development. This implies that they create specific funding components and acknowledge that the fostering of partnerships and building of institutions and capacities are always long-term commitments.

Elements which strengthen these efforts include, among other aspects, (i) the earmarking of credit shares and the allocation of budget-related competencies to the partners, (ii) the provision of finance for publications, (iii) the facilitating of access to electronic networks, and (iv) the integration of Southern researchers in management boards of donor agencies.

In order to promote effective partnerships, funding agencies are expected not to make any compromises. They should meet their responsibility as key players by linking any funding activity to a training/capacity-building component, to the benefit of their partners, and in addition by assuring a consistent monitoring which includes criteria for assessing the potential and effectiveness of communication and the extent of collaborative efforts and real partnership.

The following triangle illustrates the articulation of the key components to be evaluated

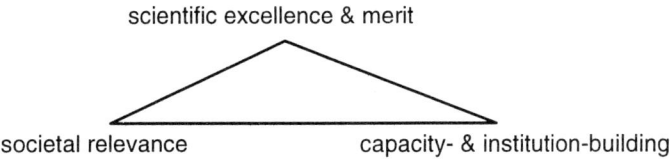

- *National political bodies* in the North and South need to commit themselves to research as one component of national and global development and development cooperation. This reorientation of the policy framework is a basic condition for the emergence of any committed and effective research collaboration. An appropriate policy framework will lead to research agendas which are governed by demand, address relevant common concerns, and consider all the actors involved.

* * *

The authors are confident that the current discussion of partnership concepts is going in the right direction. It is now clearly recognised that enhanced and genuine North-South research partnership is called upon to play a pivotal role in the drive to address concerns regarding our common future effectively. The deliberations at the Conference, with the outlook they provided, assure us that we have moved from a state of talking and thinking together towards the crucial phase of acting and developing together. In this respect, the creation of a favourable policy framework remains the critical issue. Once the new approaches for North-South research partnerships have taken root, they will make a contribution to the establishment of a new style of international scientific cooperation, characterised by committed and effective research partnerships.

References

Bangura, Y. Who defines, who pushes and who funds research agendas in the South? Introduction to the Working Groups A1 and A2.

Castillo, G. Research Partnerships: Issues, Lessons, Results and Dreams for Sustainable Development. Manuscript for the introductory session.

Fogelberg, T. Concepts of Research Partnership. Round Table Statement.

Geiser, U. Research Agendas. Report of the Working Group A2

Hardie, J.D.M. Research Partnerships and Sustainable Development. Some Contextual Reflections. Handout summarising the introductory speech.

Hountondji, P.J. Equity in reward systems: Ownership and value of data and results. Introduction to Working Group F.
Korte, R. Research Competition in Developing Countries. Contribution to the Panel Discussion.
Mokhele, K., Forster, J. South-South Collaboration. Report of the Working Group D.
OECD. Shaping the 21st Century: The contribution of development cooperation. OECD Paper DCD/DAC(96)15.
RAWOO 1995. Towards a European Science & Technology Policy for Development: Issues and Options. The Hague.
RAWOO 1995. Supporting capacity building for research in the South. Recommendations for Dutch policy. The Hague.
Wils, F. 1995. Building up and strengthening research capacity in Southern countries. RAWOO Publication no. 9, The Hague.

All these manuscripts and reports have been submitted to the Conveners of the Conference. Copies are available, on request, from the KFPE Secretariat.

Promoting Research Capacities in Developing Countries and Countries in Transition: The Contribution of SDC

Urs Herren

The Swiss Agency for Development and Cooperation (SDC) is a part of the Federal Department of Foreign Affairs. It is responsible for technical assistance and a larger part of the financial aid for both developing countries and countries in transition in Central and Eastern Europe. It handles about 75 per cent of all Swiss official development assistance (ODA) under the Federal law of 1976 on international development assistance and humanitarian aid.

Under this law, SDC has the mandate to contribute to the building of research capacities in its partner countries and to promote relevant scientific research and academic training in Switzerland. This mandate is based on the conviction that the central problems of development cannot be tackled, and sustainable development cannot be reached, without a significant strengthening of the capacity of all countries - North, South and East - to define and scientifically investigate the problems they confront.

The objectives of research promotion

In order to improve the coherence of its activities in the field of research and science (R&S), SDC adopted a *Research Promotion Policy* in 1993. It has two central objectives:

- to strengthen independent research capacities in partner countries;
- to contribute towards solving priority development problems;

and two subsidiary objectives:

- to improve the activities of Swiss development assistance;
- to promote Swiss research relevant to developing countries and countries in transition.

SDC is convinced that today, independent research capacities in the South and East are crucial, not least to confront problems which are of common and global concern. These can only be addressed by joint research efforts involving scientists from all parts of the globe.

SDC expenditure on science and research activities

SDC is currently investing about CHF 45 million per year for the promotion of research and science (R&S) activities. This corresponds to about 6 per cent of the SDC development cooperation budget, and to slightly less than 4 per cent of total Swiss official development assistance.

The following table shows how these funds are allocated:

Annual SDC expenditure for R&S activities	CHF Mio.	%
a) Contributions within bilateral country or sector programmes	21	46
b) Contributions to multilateral research programmes	16	36
c) Contributions to the academic training of Swiss scientists	5	11
d) Contributions to partnership programmes between research institutions in Switzerland and the South/East	3	7
TOTAL	**45**	**100**

a) Contributions within bilateral projects and programmes

Almost half of the total funds SDC invests for the promotion of R&S activities are allocated within country or sector programmes. Projects are of a wide variety of types, ranging from support to national and regional universities, to specific research projects and regional or thematic scientific networks. These projects are largely based on specific needs in the South and the main partners of SDC are, in most cases, research institutions are involved in a considerable number of projects and programmes (corresponding to a volume of about CHF 18 million), whether as implementing agencies, with specific research, backstopping or training mandates, or in a consultative capacity.

b) Contributions to multilateral research programmes

About a third of R&S expenditure contributes to multilateral research programmes. Given SDC's focus on poorer countries and regions with an agricultural base, most of these funds are channelled through the International Agricultural Research Centres of the Consultative Group for International Agricultural Research (CGIAR). It may also be noted that about 40 per cent of the total R&S expenditure of SDC deals with issues of sustainable agriculture and natural resource management.

c) Contributions to the academic training of Swiss scientists

In order to enable Swiss research to contribute positively to the aims of SDC's research promotion policy, SDC is promoting the academic training of young Swiss scientists in development issues and supports a number of competence centres within Switzerland. It is interested in the growing integration of Swiss research in international scientific collaboration, especially with developing countries and the countries of central and eastern Europe.

About CHF 5 million per year is invested in the academic training of young researchers, both by supporting specific training institutes, like the Institut Universitaire d'Etudes du Développement (IUED) in Geneva, the Postgraduate Course on Developing Countries (NADEL) at the Federal Institute of Technology in Zurich and the Postgraduate Cycle on Development at the Federal Institute of Technology in Lausanne, and by allocating individual grants to young researchers.

d) Promoting research partnerships between R&S institutions in Switzerland and in developing and transition countries

Since 1991, a more intensive dialogue has taken place between development agencies and the Swiss research funding institutions. A joint effort of the Swiss Academy of Natural Sciences and SDC has led to the formulation of a Swiss *Strategy for the Promotion of Research with Developing Countries* (1993). It started from the fact that Swiss research in and on developing countries financed with research funds was in a marginal position, that projects were mainly small, scattered and highly selective, and finally, that the large majority paid little attention to questions of societal relevance or capacity-building.

As a first step, the Swiss Commission for Research Partnership with Developing Countries (KFPE), which has organised the present Conference, was established to improve the dialogue between the development and research communities, and to promote further the partnership approach in all domains of research funding in Switzerland. This approach is based on the conviction that it is possible, by initiating longer-term partnerships between research institutions in the North and South, to achieve both relevant research results and a capacity-building effect on both sides.

In the period 1996-99, SDC is contributing towards two pilot initiatives by jointly funding partnership programmes in strategic research domains together with the main Swiss research funding agency, the Swiss National Science Foundation (SNSF):

- <u>Environmental research</u>: SDC and SNSF are each contributing around CHF 1.5 million for the module *Development and Environment* within the Priority Programme Environment of the SNSF. Only projects conceived as research partnerships and addressing relevant development issues qualify for funding.

Part III The contribution of Swiss Development Cooperation

- Research cooperation with eastern European countries: around CHF 1.2 million per year is invested in cooperation projects between Swiss and host country research institutions, which combine research and capacity-building objectives.

SDC highly commends the recent approval of a strategy paper by the SNSF which underlines the responsibility of the Swiss research community for promoting research collaboration with developing countries. As was announced at the Conference, SDC is ready for further joint efforts to develop research partnerships with both developing and transition countries.

Documentation

SDC Research Promotion Policy, 1993 (available at SDC, Policy and Research Section, CH-3003 Bern, Switzerland).

Swiss Research and Developing Countries 1996, IUED, 1993/94 (available on floppy disk and CD-ROM at Institut Universitaire d' Etudes du Développement, P.O. Box 136, CH-1211 Genève 21, Switzerland).

The Swiss National Science Foundation and Research for Development

Beat Sottas

Previous studies (e.g. IUED 1996, Sottas 1993) have shown that the Swiss National Science Foundation (SNSF) plays a considerable role in supporting Swiss-based research in developing countries. In comparison to the whole budget of Switzerland's most important public funding agency for the sponsoring of research, the amount spent in the domain of research for development might appear small. However, there are good reasons to believe that this sponsoring has an impact that reaches beyond the grants allocated: firstly, it allows young researchers to carry out a study with the aim of obtaining an academic degree; secondly, the fact that a project is accepted for a grant is generally seen as the acknowledgement of good scientific standards; thirdly, though many of the projects funded are small, they are extremely varied. This enables knowledge and scientific capacity to be sustained and increased over a wide array of disciplines. Furthermore, such projects enable individuals carrying out research in or with developing countries to develop their own abilities and scientific reputation. Grants from SNSF are thus important for the personal careers of Swiss scientists, but they also help to ensure that in Swiss universities and research institutions there will be competent scientists who have experience of the problems of the developing world.

This brief outline raises some questions regarding the prevailing expectations as compared to the goals of the SNSF. In order to understand the practices it may be helpful first to outline the mandate and the principles of Switzerland's most important public research funding agency.

The Swiss National Science Foundation was established in 1952 as a private foundation. Mandated by the Swiss Government, it is entrusted with the promotion of non-commercial scientific research at Swiss universities and other scientific institutions.

In 1995, the Foundation had about 325 million Swiss francs at its disposal. The priorities are reflected in the proportions of the funds allocated to groups of disciplines: approximately 40% is earmarked for mathematics, sciences and engineering, another 40% is foreseen for medicine and biology, and the humanities and social sciences are allocated a share of slightly less than 20% of the Foundation's annual budget.

One of the main goals is to support a sufficiently large number of qualified scientists in all the disciplines; they are expected to constitute the critical mass which maintains and improves the standards in research and teaching at Swiss universities in a long term perspective. Projects funded by the SNSF cover a maximum period of three years. Besides the hundreds of small projects and a relatively small number of large projects running in parallel, up to now the SNSF has launched more than 40 National Research Programmes aimed at finding solutions to prevailing problems in the state, society and culture. Basically, these programmes address a broad range of issues of general interest to the country. In recent years, this scope has been enlarged by launching the so-called Priority Programmes which aim at strengthening Swiss research in specific scientific areas of strategic importance. Currently, four Federal Priority Programmes are running under the auspices of the SNSF and three are being executed by the Board of the Swiss Federal Institutes of Technology.

At present, the concept of research partnership is receiving a lot of attention in the international scientific community. As the Berne Conference showed, this reflects an increased awareness among industrialised countries of the need to adopt appropriate strategies to tackle common societal and environmental concerns. The main funding agency of the country is exposed to this conceptual shift as well, and consequently there is some pressure for a stronger orientation towards research partnerships.

However, the support of Swiss basic research is the SNSF's statutory main task, and the problem of capacity-building in developing countries is generally considered to be the concern of development cooperation. Consequently, the SNSF only supports Swiss research groups. Funds for potential research partners from developing countries and for specific capacity-building measures have to be requested from SDC, the Swiss Agency for Development and Cooperation. This situation led to the launching of Module 7, Development & Environment, of the Priority Programme Environment, which is jointly financed by SNSF and SDC. Besides this, an important commitment towards developing countries is the membership in the International Foundation for Science, in Stockholm, which supports young, promising scientists from developing countries. The SNSF has supported this foundation substantially since 1977.

The following table refers to 125 grants allocated to research projects and other scientific activities identified as having a potential link to research in developing countries (thematically or topically related, the research being executed in a developing country, or including collaborators from the South). The table is based on SNSF's annual reports 1993-1995. The information in the reports is not sufficiently detailed to allow a precise and comprehensive sampling; nevertheless, the table clearly shows the prevailing trends, and illustrates the practices and the commitment with regard to developing countries.

Category of Grant	1993	1994	1995	Total	partnership-oriented
Div. 1: Humanities	5	8	11	24	max. 6
Div. 2: Sciences & Engineering	3	6	5	14	+/- 0
Div. 3: Medicine & Biology	6	6	6	18	max. 2
Div. 4: Special Programmes	17	4	1	22	approx. 20
Young researchers	-	7	20	27	approx. 16
Publications	1	4	-	5	max. 3
Scientific conferences	10	1	4	15	approx. 1

Projects of Divisions 1 to 3, supporting Swiss basic research, rarely fit into the concept of research partnership. Indeed, most of them have just a thematic relation to developing countries, the beneficiaries being primarily Swiss researchers or research teams. The 22 projects of Division 4 mainly correspond to the above-mentioned Module 7, Development & Environment, of the Priority Programme Environment. With this module the SNSF, together with SDC, tried for the first time to integrate the idea of research partnership into a part of its funding activities. However, aside from the Module 7 projects where collaboration with partners from the South and capacity-building there was a prerequisite, Swiss research in developing countries seems to be largely an enterprise exporting data and knowledge from the South, with a very limited impact on capacity-building there.

This situation is partly due to a general policy deficit as well as to structural and organisational deficits within the management of individual projects. Given the mandate of SNSF to further capacity-building exclusively within Switzerland, there was no room for the elaboration of instruments to support capacity-building outside the country. This explains the situation which systematically created unilateral benefits. In fact, with the exception of a very limited number of individual projects and one module of the Priority Programme Environment, a partnership approach was rarely the basis of any collaboration. Moreover, there was no necessity to practise partnership and also no means to enforce a more equilibrated state. Furthermore, SNSF had no possibility of facilitating the emergence of a centre of excellence to carry out research for development.

The intensified discussion about genuine research partnership with developing countries reflects the recognition that the scientific community has to play a major role in meeting the overwhelming challenges that developing countries face. The SNSF has acknowledged this conceptual shift, and in its four-year programme for 1996-1999 it has declared its willingness to assume its responsibility, as the major Swiss funding agency, to participate in efforts to strengthen the international research collaboration with developing countries - provided that political and financial support for this concern continues. Some promising first steps have been undertaken. Recently, the SNSF adopted another long-term commitment to the International Foundation of Science. Furthermore, it decided to examine the feasibility and usefulness of an institutional partnership with a sister organisation in a developing country in order to support capacity-building in science administration. Finally, preparations are under way to promote to a limited extent joint research projects submitted by representatives from the North and the South, not only within Module 7, but also within the SNSF's normal research funding activities (Divisions 1 to 3). This funding activity will probably be operational from 1997 onward. Such research partnership projects will have to consist of a joint Swiss/developing country consortium, though applications for the whole consortium can only be made by researchers attached to an institution based in Switzerland and not directly by scientists originating from a deve-loping country.

All these measures make it apparent that the SNSF acknowledges the important role that science plays with regard to sustainable development, and accordingly is moving towards a more active engagement in research in and with developing countries.

References

IUED 1996. Swiss Research in Developing Countries. IUED, Geneva.

Sottas, B. 1994. Perspektiven für Afrikastudien in der Schweiz. Eine Evaluation des aktuellen Standes und ein Modell zur künftigen Ausgestaltung. FER 151/1994. Schweizerischer Wissenschaftsrat, Bern. 107 Seiten.

Swiss National Science Foundation. Annual Reports 1993-1995. Bern.

The author wishes to thank Dr. Jürg Pfister from the Swiss National Science Foundation for the information regarding the foundation's future activities encouraging research for development.

Part III　　　　　　　　　　　　　　Contributions to the Conference

Conference Programme Overview

Tuesday, 5 March 1996
Introductory Sessions & Overview of Experience Gained in Research Partnership - Voices from the South and the North

Opening Addresses
Christoph Schäublin, Rector of the University of Berne
Flavio Cotti, Federal Councillor of Switzerland, Department of Foreign Affairs, Berne

Chairman morning sessions: ***Thierry A. Freyvogel***, President, Swiss Commission for Research Partnership with Developing Countries (KFPE) & Chairman Organising Committee, Basle

Introductions: *Research Partnership - its Potential for Sustainable Development*
Gelia Castillo, College of Agriculture, University of the Philippines, Los Banos, Philippines
John Hardie, Director Policy and Planning, International Development Research Centre (IDRC), Ottawa, Canada
Bruno Messerli, Co-director Past Global Changes (PAGES), Coordinator UNU-Programme and Member KFPE, University of Berne

Keynote Address: *Research Capacities Needed*
Mohamed Hag Ali Hassan, Executive Director Third World Academy of Sciences (TWAS), Trieste, Italy

Chairman afternoon sessions: ***Jean-Luc Maurer***, Director Graduate Institute of Development Studies (IUED), Member Organising Committee and KFPE, Geneva

Round Table: *Concepts of Research Partnership*
Moderator: ***Rolf Probala***, Head News Department, Swiss Broadcasting Corporation, Zurich
Participants:
Rolf Carlman, Director Department for Research Co-operation SAREC - SIDA, Stockholm, Sweden

Teresa Fogelberg, Head Research Programme, Directorate General for Development Co-operation (DGIS), Ministry of Foreign Affairs, The Hague, The Netherlands
Martin Khor, Research Director, Consumers Association of Penang, Pulau Pinang, Malaysia
Bakary Ouayogodé, Research Director, Department of Education and Scientific Research, Abidjan, Côte d'Ivoire
Last minute regrets from:
Mambillikalathil Govind Kumar Menon, M.P., former Chairman Committee on Science and Technology in Developing Countries & International Biosciences Networks (COSTED/IBN), New Delhi, India (not replaced)

Keynote Address:*The Contribution of Research to Sustainable Development*
Uma Lele, Advisor, Agricultural Research, Environmentally Sustainable Development, International Bank for Reconstruction and Development ('World Bank'), Washington D.C., USA
Last minute regrets from:
Moctar Touré, Executive Secretary, Special Program for Agricultural Research (SPAAR), International Bank for Reconstruction and Development ('World Bank'), Washington D.C., USA (replaced by Uma Lele)

Wednesday, 6 March 1996
Collaborative Efforts for a Better Partnership

Panel Discussion: *International Competition for Research in the South - International Programmes and the Experiences of Different Partners*
Moderator: *John Howell*, Director, Overseas Development Institute (ODI), London, United Kingdom
Participants:
Christian Bonte-Friedheim, General Director International Service for National Agricultural Research (ISNAR), The Hague, The Netherlands
Jacques Charmes, "Institut français de recherche scientifique pour le développement en coopération" (ORSTOM), Paris, France

Rolf Korte, Head Department for Health, Population and Nutrition, "Deutsche Gesellschaft für technische Zusammenarbeit" (GTZ), Eschborn, Germany
Hugo Romero, Head Graduate School, School of Architecture and Urbanism, University of Santiago, Chile
Leena Srivastava, Dean, Policy Analysis Division, TATA Research Institute, New Delhi, India
Last minute regrets from
George Benneh, Vice-Chancellor University of Ghana, Legon, Ghana (not replaced)

Forum: *Swiss Policy in Partnership*
Moderator: ***Jean-Philippe Rapp***, Moderator, Swiss Broadcasting Corporation (SRG), Geneva
Representatives of Swiss politics:
Bernard Comby, National Councillor, Member Swiss National Council and KFPE, Saxon
Hans Rudolf Nebiker, National Councillor, Member Swiss National Council, Diegten
Thomas Onken, Councillor of States, Member Swiss Council of States, Solothurn
Rosemarie Simmen, Councillor of States, Member Swiss Council of States, Solothurn
Representatives of Swiss institutions concerned with research:
André Aeschlimann, President Research Council of the Swiss National Science Foundation (SNSF), Berne
Jean-François Giovannini, Vice-Director Swiss Agency for Development and Co-operation (SDC), Berne
Bruno Messerli, Co-director Past Global Changes (PAGES), Coordinator UNU-Program and Member KFPE, University of Berne
Francis Waldvogel, President, Council of the Federal Institutes of Technology, University of Geneva
Last minute regrets from
Barbara Haering Binder, National Councillor, Member Swiss National Council, Zurich (ZH) (replaced by Thomas Onken)

Wednesday, 6 March 1996 continued

Poster Session & Lunch-Buffet

Working Groups

A   Research Agendas - Who Defines, who Pays, who Pushes them and what are the Expected Results and Benefits? Priorities of Research as seen from the South
Initiator: **Yusuf Bangura**, Research Coordinator United Nations Research Institute for Social Development (UNRISD), Geneva; Co-Moderators A1: **Frederick W.B. Bugenyi**, Fisheries Research Institute (FIRI), Jinja, Uganda & **Richard Gerster**, Director Swiss Coalition of Development Organizations and Member KFPE, Berne; Co-Moderators A2: **Urs Geiser**, Department of Geography, University of Zurich & **Martin Khor**, Research Director, Consumers Association of Penang, Pulau Pinang, Malaysia

B   Pitfalls of Partnership - Covered Leadership, Data for Donations ...
Initiator: **Ruth Egger**, Sector Head "Intercoopération" (IC) & Member KFPE, Berne; Co-Moderators: **Oumar Niangado**, Former Director Cinzana Agricultural Research Station, General Director "Institut d'économie rurale", Bamako, Mali & **Stephen C. Stearns**, University of Basle, Switzerland

C   Constraints on Research Partnership - Institutional, Structural, Financial and Discipline-related Aspects
Initiator: **K.N. Nair**, Centre for Development Studies, Thiruvananthapuram, India; Co-Moderators: **George King'oriah**, Deputy Vice-Chancellor, Egerton University, Kenya & **Peter Rieder**, President Swiss Centre for International Agriculture (ZIL) and Member KFPE, Zurich

D   South-South Research Collaboration - Potentials and Hindrances
Initiator: **Jorge Eduardo Allende**, Head Biochemical Department, University of Chile, Santiago, Chile; Co-Moderators: **Jacques Forster**, Graduate Institute of Development Studies (IUED) and Member KFPE, Geneva & **Khotso Mokhele**, Foundation for Research Development, Pretoria, South Africa

E   Aims of Capacity and Institution Building - Expectations and Strategies
Initiator: **Roland Waast**, "Institut français de recherche scientifique pour le développement en coopération" (ORSTOM), Paris, France;

Part III Conference Program Overview

Co-Moderators: **Dyna Carol Arhin**, Lecturer Health Economics & Financing Programme, London School of Hygiene & Tropical Medicine, UK & **Roland Schertenleib**, Swiss Federal Institute for Environment Science and Technology (EAWAG) and Member KFPE, Dübendorf

F   Equity in Reward Systems - Ownership and Value of Data and Results

Initiator: **Paulin A. Hountondji**, Former Minister, Philosopher, University of Benin, Cotonou, Benin; Co-Moderators: **Gueladio Cissé**, "Ecole interétats d'ingénieurs de l'équipement rural", Ouagadougou, Burkina Faso & **Jean-Bernard Dubois**, Swiss Agency for Development and Co-operation (SDC), Berne;

G   Transfer of Findings - Effects Towards Local Populations, Centres of Excellence & National Policies

Initiator: **Lotfia El Nadi**, National Institute of Laser Enhanced Studies (NILES), Cairo University, Giza, Egypt & University of Qatar, Doha; Co-Moderators: **Francis Ndegwa Gichuki**, Agricultural Engineer, University of Nairobi, Kenya & **Marcel Tanner**, Vice-Director Swiss Tropical Institute (STI) and Member KFPE, Basle

H   Access to Knowledge and Results - Facing Remoteness of Researchers in the South

Initiator: **Bui Thi Lang**, Chief Department, Committee for Science and Technology, Environmental Committee (ENCO), Ho Chi Minh City, Vietnam; Co-Moderators: **Rudolf Baumgartner**, Postgraduate Course on Developing Countries (NADEL) and Member KFPE, Zurich & **Emmanuel Ndione**, Director Environment and Development for Africa (ENDA), responsible for Sahel and West-Africa, Dakar, Senegal & **Carol Priestley**, International Africa Institute (IAI), London, United Kingdom

I   Le rôle de l'intermédiation de la recherche pour le développement (French-speaking working group)

Initiator: **Gerda Fellay**, Association Jeunesse et Parents Conseils (AJPC), Lausanne; Co-Moderators: **Mohammed Naciri**, Université Mohammed V, Rabat, Morocco & **Jean-Marie Plancherel**, CFRC Coopération, Federal Institute of Technology (EPFL) and Member KFPE, Lausanne

Thursday, 7 March 1996
Commitment to a Partnership-Agenda

Co-Chairpersons morning sessions: **Maria Antonietta Camacho**, Environmental Sociologist, Universidad Nacional Heredia, Heredia, Costa Rica & **Ruedi Högger**, President Helvetas, Swiss Association for International Cooperation, Zurich

Group Reports by Co-moderators of the Working Groups

Chairman afternoon sessions: **Hans Rudolf Thierstein**, Chairman Expert Group Swiss Priority Programme Environment (SPPE) of the Swiss National Science Foundation (SNSF), Swiss Federal Institute of Technology (ETHZ), Zurich

Keynote Address: *The Private Sector and Research Partnership*
Kohn Michael, Chairman Institute for "Capital & Economy", Hon. Chairman International Chamber of Commerce (ICC), Zurich

Executive Summary
Ana Maria Cetto, University of Mexico City, Vice Chair Committee on Science and Technology in Developing Countries & the International Biosciences Networks (COSTED/IBN), University of Mexico, Mexico City
Thierry A. Freyvogel, President Swiss Commission for Research Partnership with Developing Countries (KFPE) & Chairman Organising Committee, Basle
Naigzi Gebremedhin, Coordinator National Environmental Action Plan, Ministry of Agriculture, Asmara, Eritrea
Raquel V. Francisco, Philippine Atmospheric, Geophysical, and Astronomical Services Administration (PAGASA), Quezon City, Philippines

Closing of the Conference
Walter Fust, Director Swiss Agency for Development and Cooperation (SDC), Berne

compiled by Daniel Maselli

Research Partnership - its Potential for Sustainable Development
Summary of the Introductory Addresses

Flavio Cotti, Federal Councillor of Switzerland, Department of Foreign Affairs, Berne

Gelia T. Castillo, Prof. emerit., College of Agriculture, University of the Philippines, Los Baños (The Philippines)

John D.M. Hardie, Director Policy and Planning, International Development Research Centre (IDRC), Ottawa (Canada)

Bruno Messerli, Co-director Past Global Changes (PAGES), Co-ordinator UNU-Programme, University of Berne

In his opening address, Federal Councillor **Flavio Cotti,** who opened the event, said he saw the Conference evolving from the "Spirit of Rio". The Rio Conference has clearly launched a new era because the destiny of future generations has been set as the benchmark for all current human activities. The emphasis on the tremendous challenge of reaching and maintaining sustainable development constitutes a new paradigm. Switzerland has recognised the importance of the issue. Accordingly, it has committed itself to a stronger international solidarity and collaboration for sustainable development. Among other steps, it has ratified the conventions on climate and biodiversity. Moreover, it has taken up the theme by promoting the achievement of the objectives formulated in Agenda 21.

In the processes and changes needed for a sustainable future, research plays a key role. However, there is no doubt that considerable efforts are still necessary to comprehend the complexity of the prevailing problems and to find appropriate solutions.

To reach these goals, Councillor Cotti stressed that it is of crucial importance for all countries to be able to identify and the study problems they are confronted with, using their own resources. However, self-reliant problem solving is jeopardised by a number of unfavourable conditions. Despite considerable differences among the various developing countries - poorer regions of Africa and Asia compared to the newly industrialised countries - disparities between North and South prevail and structural dissimilarities are far from being solved. In general, the gap between the capacities of the North and the South is widening, the ratio between the number of qualified scientists and engineers and the total number of inhabitants is very different (e.g. 100 per million in Africa, but 3500 per million in OECD countries). Financial, scientific and technological dependency on the North is constantly increasing. The possibility of joining the "global information highway" is not affordable, and the status of scientists remains as low as their incomes, which further accelerates the "brain drain".

Research activities in collaboration with developing countries have a long tradition in Switzerland. A recent survey came up with a list of almost 400 projects, involving 250 Swiss institutions. However, many of these projects tend to be small, selective and limited to one discipline. Given this situation, which does not often produce long-lasting effects in the South, Switzerland (or more precisely the Swiss Agency for Development and Cooperation) favours strategies which opt for the creation of independent research capacities. Consequently, Swiss development assistance supports - often through the channels of multilateral networks - academic training and scientific research in developing countries. With respect to the reaching of these goals, Swiss researchers and research institutions play a minor role for they participate in only about one quarter of these activities. In short, the underlying concept of research partnership aims at joining the concerns of both research and development policy.

After this opening address, which summarised the Swiss position, Professor **Gelia T. Castillo** gave an introduction to research partnership which focused on the issues and the results, and also the lessons to be drawn on the way to achieving the dream of sustainable development. Although she observes a "partnership syndrome" which currently preoccupies the international scientific community, partnership can only function if a number of requirements are fulfilled at various levels. Based on her long experience in the domain of agricultural research, she illustrated the various aspects of research partnership using the example of rice research. Given the fact that rice is the basic food for nearly half of the people on earth, she has found that - especially in Asia - talking about rice is very often synonymous with talking about development.

To start off a sound and comprehensive discussion of the theme of the Conference, Professor Castillo wanted the audience to think about eight aspects of research partnership:

A) The case for research partnership
B) The grey side of partnership
C) North-South and South-South partnerships
D) Capacity-strengthening and transaction costs of partnerships
E) Interdisciplinarity
F) Choosing research partners
G) Partnerships that promise to make a difference
H) Dreaming dreams for sustainability and a common future

A) The case for research partnership
At present, all parties involved in North-South research activities are being urged to complete the transition from a donor-client partnership approach to one of equal partnership. Given the fact that without the three key concepts of participation, partnership and sustainability no international development can proceed or even be started, these ideas have to become the modi operandi of all ongoing activities.

There are practical reasons for partnership. During a time of diminishing research support strong partnerships will allow for the harnessing of all available resources. In practice, one could think of a research consortium approach. This model starts from shared responsibilities, making the best possible use of the comparative advantages of each participant, such as capacities, facilities, knowledge, and human resources. Thus, problems as well as opportunities are partitioned among international and national centres of excellence.

In sum, the following are arguments in favour of the partnership approach:
- collaboration between groups with different experience can lead to greater efficiency in dealing with increasingly heterogeneous environments
- it can lead to greater effectiveness in finding sustainable solutions for specific locations
- broader insights promote relevance, and can mobilise the conscience of science to meet or share the responsibilities
- partnerships are a response to increased political awareness, which demands equality and the overcoming of dependencies with unilateral benefits
- it is, last but not least, an appropriate response to declining research funds.

B) The grey side of partnership
Despite the ethical and scientific rationale for research partnership, the existence of the following "unhealthy" types of partnership must not be swept under the carpet:
- partnerships of convenience - where partners in the South function simply to legitimise researchers from elsewhere entering a country
- contractual partnership - where partners from the South gather the data while interested parties in the North pay for the services and own the data. Research then becomes a data-exporting enterprise with minimal building of research capability
- uneven division of labour - where the North proposes the project, develops the procedure and finds the funds. In such a non-partnering-partnership the South implements the research, but knowledge and prestige are transferred to the North
- reluctant partnerships with reluctant partners - where the main preoccupation is how to take advantage of resources available on either side
- patronage - where the Southern partner is assigned the role of a minor associate and has to endure paternalism and continuous advice.

In fairness, it must also be said that there can be exploitation of the North by the South. Funds may be misappropriated, facts misrepresented and powers and resources misused. Some scientists from the South, based in the North and enjoying the advantages of working there, still pass themselves off as representatives from the South. Some receive funds and travel abroad, but never submit reports.

C) North-South, South-South and other partnerships
Traditionally, research collaboration developed from patterns of colonial history. New dimensions emerged with the advent of large international programmes. However, even in such a setting, national or regional partners have to prove that there is some measurable impact for funding to continue. At present, the pinnacle of research partnership is North-South; efforts in the South are barely acknowledged if they are not practically and intellectually integrated into so-called world-class research, as defined by the North.

With regional developments and political alliances between the advanced South, the developing South and the least developed South, South-South collaboration has become more fashionable. However, this horizontal sharing - rather ironically - is more often than not dependent on donors from the North. In this way, the South risks the perpetuation of being accorded only second-class research status. On the other hand, it is a commonplace that those who bring good money do not always bring good ideas. Research partnership requires mutuality of benefits.

D) Research capacity-strengthening and the transaction costs of partnerships

Joint and equal partnerships need capacity-building, otherwise they will become what has been called "parachuting science". However, experience has repeatedly shown that it is easier to build than to utilise and maintain capacity. The international community is rich in experience of capacity building, but seems to suffer from an "intellectual immunity to cross-learning", especially between sectors - agriculture is slow to learn from health research and vice versa. Castillo emphasised the importance of learning research by doing research, i.e. combining training and research and adopting institution-strengthening approaches around talented individuals. She quoted some examples where the key determinants of productive research and capacity-building are clearly demonstrated. Southern partners must have sufficient scientific skills, personality and leadership to be able to say "yes" or "no" to any potential associate; therefore, purely academic qualifications are not good indicators for failure or success. Moreover, exchange with institutions abroad is crucial for the updating of knowledge. However, there is an inherent danger that individuals who possess all the necessary qualifications suffer from over-commitment, e.g. they undertake consultancies to earn more money, and are involved in multiple partnerships to foster promising networks.

These aspects show already that research partnerships are likely to have considerable transaction costs. Time is probably the most prominent: it takes time to design and consolidate institutional arrangements, to obtain clearances, to negotiate and re-negotiate roles and responsibilities, to mobilise funds, to train people and get reports. It is often easier to get international partnerships organised than to persuade institutions within a country to leave their own closely-guarded "turf" and work together. Here, an external body can act as a catalyst to encourage collaboration - or as a dividing wedge pushing institutions further apart. In establishing partnerships it is often difficult to offer adequate incentive structures in terms of research careers and balanced financial rewards - but we should not wait until the criteria for ideal partnership can be fulfilled before embarking on projects in partnership.

E) Interdisciplinarity

Every research partnership claims to be interdisciplinary. In many instances, however, interdisciplinarity is restricted to the biological and physical sciences. The inclusion or exclusion of social sciences is, therefore, a serious issue. It seems that some researchers are still intimidated by the complexity of human behaviour. This state of affairs is most regrettable because experience has repeatedly shown that there is indeed a potent rationale for including non-biophysical aspects. For example the promise of agricultural technologies has often not been fulfilled due a lack of attention to the wider cultural context as well as to increased production. Ultimately, research has to be directed in the light of the "research-adoption-impact continuum". It is for this reason too, that farmer-participatory, gender-sensitive, user-responsive and farmer-researcher partnerships have been advocated. In integrated pest management, this shift has been stimulated by the input of social scientists who have emphasised the managerial, psychological and social aspects, or the general acceptance of research. Those who succeeded with the "paradigm shift" involved in the joint efforts were apparently not intimidated by the complexity of human behaviour.

F) Choosing research partners
Besides North-South and South-South patterns, one has to examine the issue of partnership between the weak and the strong. As pointed out in a study sponsored by CGIAR (Consultative Group on International Agricultural Research), research centres in the South are seen as "lamentably weak". Even in the case of the CGIAR network, several decades of institution-strengthening efforts and large investments by bilateral and multilateral donors have not changed this situation. Even if this estimation downplays the power of the well established global organisation, it is obvious that universities which suffer from chronic lack of money, political pressure, and brain drain, operate under incomparably more difficult conditions. The perception is widespread that national research systems are like "empty vessels" meant to catch manna from heaven, instead of seeing them as systems with needs and assets of their own to contribute to research partnership. Of the three options - substitution, by-passing or strengthening - Castillo emphasised that strengthening is necessary and the only viable alternative.

In this context, she quoted authors who associate the prevailing weak state of organisation in the South with the blue-print model of institution-strengthening as "a linear process of going through stages of development" with defined indicators. In such a setting, aspects of partnering are often ignored. Priority is given to a set of desired outcomes and the establishment of benchmarks regarding results, structures and services. This contradicts the ideals of participatory development and adversely affects true partnership, which is characterised by a mutuality of responsibilities and benefits.

G) Partnerships that promise to make a difference
Given the fact that functioning partnership is not primarily a matter of institutional arrangements but involves a complex chemistry of personalities and cross-cultural encounters, several modalities are able to facilitate and promote the planned or ongoing venture. Besides bilateral arrangements between researchers and organisations, shuttle research, networks and consortia all promise to make a difference. Shuttle research based on mutual exchange between sites in the North and the South consolidates friendships and creates personal commitments.

Networks, on the other hand, are more informal with an almost unlimited participation by interested persons and organisations. However, they often take time before they really lead to synergies. Moreover, there is a tendency towards a centre-periphery conflict, with power differentials and a "hub and spoke" interaction between the co-ordinating office and the periphery. This does not facilitate the development of relations and capacity building across the network.

A consortium has some comparative advantages because it is formally organised among a limited number of involved institutions. They agree on a common research agenda with clearly defined areas of responsibility, division of labour and sharing of resources.

Professor Castillo then briefly described six case studies from the field of agricultural research. One may learn four lessons: 1) partnerships between "local experts" and "global experts", who jointly identify local needs and problems, are able to seek solutions locally and globally, based on local understanding and international expertise; 2) social science research plays a significant role in developing research priorities and in assessing the impact of changes; 3) there is a clear recognition that not even the most brilliant scientist can do it alone - in many domains it is even becoming the norm that those who are not inclined to share are denied access to further support; 4) problem-oriented research has to be opened beyond the barriers of disciplines - pluridisciplinary approaches with a holistic perspective are compulsory, e.g. the assessment of whether agricultural technologies help or hurt poor women has to be done in a holistic sense rather than within the confines of the farming operations under question.

H) Dreaming dreams for sustainability and our common future

Professor Castillo concluded that research partnerships foster a global science which unites humankind across cultures, countries, ideologies, disciplines and personalities. In search of sustainability, research partnerships forge an alliance with indigenous knowledge, whereby even the weak can contribute to the potential and efforts of the strong. A promising example is the UPWARD network (User's Perspective with Agricultural Research and Development) in six Asian countries, which promotes and facilitates partnerships between "local" experts and "global" experts, who jointly identify local needs and problems and seek solutions based on an appropriate understanding of local circumstances. Similar attempts are, among others, the RF Program on Rice Biotechnology, the Network for Genetic Evaluation of Rice (INGER), or the Women in Rice Farming Systems Research Program. Under these circumstances, research partnerships produce more than research results; they produce human relationships. Partnerships based on mutual learning and mutual respect across all skill levels create synergisms and real added value.

John D.M. Hardie from IDRC shared the same preoccupations for achieving research partnerships and he also acknowledged the necessity of a series of normative requirements. However, in order to avoid repetition he drew attention to some more basic considerations evolving from IDRC's long-lasting experience in fostering research networks in developing countries. He wanted the audience to pause for a moment's reflection on the extent of the paradigm shift in the post-war period and on the degree to which development is being rethought today. Therefore, he focused on the context in which the potential for research and research partnerships for sustainable development are located or may emerge. In his paper he outlined four contextual dimensions: knowledge in the context of development, integrating research, research in the context of the knowledge system, and effective partnerships.

Knowledge in the context of development
Dr. Hardie started his presentation with the now widely accepted assumption that development is not synonymous with economic growth. At the same time one would have to recognise that the meaning of sustainable development is still not thoroughly defined. Given this situation he saw the necessity to rethink the concept beyond environmental and economic terms. It is mainly the fact of the mutual vulnerability of all humanity and our corresponding global interdependence

which requires a comprehensive consideration along social, political and spiritual dimensions. If development is defined as a sustainable improvement in the quality of human existence, then the importance of cultural, moral and spiritual dimensions to the quality of human well-being have to be - and increasingly are being - recognised. However, this should not lead to the addition of further criteria to the assessment of development projects. Rather it is to encourage a step back from current models and to recognise the existence and interdependence of the multiple determinants of development, such as governance, culture, religion, spirituality and knowledge. The interdependence of those determinants means that if some - say governance and/or culture - are not favourable, knowledge alone will not bring about an improvement in the quality of existence. Since knowledge is the stock-in-trade of the research community, any discussion of the potential contribution of research should bear in mind that knowledge has to take its place alongside other conditions for development that may be necessary.

Integrating research
A major part of re-thinking development and research for development relates to the twin failures - or at least limited success - of the neo-classical, free market economic paradigm and the Western scientific and technological paradigm. Experience has repeatedly shown that there is no simple technological or economic fix for global problems. The practice of development has become more holistic in recent years - e.g. more integrated approaches, considering damage to biological and cultural diversity, have gained acceptance - but it is questionable whether research itself is receptive to such a shift.

The modern Western scientific enterprise has been dominated by methodologies which allowed depth at the price of fragmentation. The benefits of this reductionist approach are unquestioned, but this model is unsuitable for solving the needs of poor countries. Accordingly, it is becoming increasingly important to develop approaches that meld the natural sciences and "hard" technologies with the social sciences. The capacity to innovate technically has grown exponentially, but the equivalent capacity to devise effective forms of social institutions - e.g. viable organisational systems that permit the attainment of social goals such as equity, and appropriate policies, legislation and systems of government - lags far behind. Instead of the glamour of technology, integrated research requires other elements. It would perhaps be more appropriate to talk about "social and technical" innovation as capturing more accurately the joint imperatives that should be on the agenda.

Research in the context of the knowledge system
One way of thinking about the role of research is to consider it in the context of other components of the knowledge system: education, production of goods and services, management and organisation of institutions and enterprises, communication and information. Moreover, the non-research elements are often predominant: training, management, production, information. After all, it appears that formal research involves only a small proportion of scientists and engineers - even in industrialised countries rarely more than one-fifth are engaged in research and development.

Just as research is only one part of the knowledge system, so research itself takes a variety of forms. Especially in materially poor countries a great deal of informal research takes place: there is a largely unrewarded assortment of independent thinkers, trial and error investigators, inventors, and explorers among traditional crafts-people and rural communities.

Finally, the sub-division of the formal research sector into public and private should not be overlooked. The relationship between the two is symbiotic, but the private sector share seems to be increasing.

Effective partnerships
These contextual reflections lead to a concept of partnership that goes far beyond bilateral cooperation between two discipline-related specialists. If problems are actually to be solved, rather than theoretical solutions to be found, and if sustainable development is to occur, research partnerships should be open to a broader range of characteristics:

- multi- and (more difficult) interdisciplinarity
- participatory research modalities, involving target beneficiaries, policy-makers and other key actors (facilitating access to the fruits of informal research)
- public : private sector partnerships
- involvement of non-traditional institutions - NGOs, small and medium enterprises, local government
- close relations with other components of the knowledge system such as education, production, information, management.

Besides these criteria, Dr. Hardie emphasised that a research partnership is first and foremost an intellectual relationship and should be quite distinct from a financial joint venture. Ideally, it brings mutual benefits to all parties involved.

With the advent of modern information technologies, researchers can move much closer to the full realisation of networks as virtual research institutions, involving partners around the globe. However, the sustainability of networks is a crucial issue, because many networks are unable to maintain themselves without external support. This is particularly true in the domain of development research which requires sustained efforts. Dr. Hardie reminded all parties that it will take decades of persistent commitment.

The last introductory address was presented by Professor **Bruno Messerli**. He highlighted the potential of research partnerships for sustainable development. His arguments for the furthering of partnerships started from the point of view of the global concerns of geoscience. His presentation was subdivided into four sections: the local, national, and global context of the Conference; global research, global change, and global commons; sustainable development and research partnership; and the crucial significance of the next 30 years.

The local, national, and global context of the Conference
Professor Messerli explained first that the canton of Berne has a unique article in its constitution which not only guarantees freedom of research but also states the obligation of scientists to recognise their responsibility for sustainability in the broadest sense. He then referred to a statement on science policy by the Federal Government of Switzerland for the period 1996-1999 which pledges that the "North-South orientation of research policy in accordance with the aims set forth in Agenda 21 must be strengthened". According to him, this ultimately means that many researchers will have to accommodate to the rapidly changing priorities of the next century and must overcome the small world of personal interests, prestige, and old-fashioned structures. On a global level he asked the audience to remember the conference in Rio where Agenda 21 was devised and which tried to establish guidelines, obligations and responsibilities for the next century. Chapter 35 of the Agenda outlines two issues: first, scientists in developing countries have to be enabled to participate fully in global research programs on environment and development, and second, partnerships and open exchange of information among national, regional and global agencies have to be promoted and strengthened.

Global research, global change, and global commons
In this section Professor Messerli highlighted the contradiction between the special responsibility of the scientific community for the

global commons (atmosphere, oceans, polar regions) and the uneven distribution of capacities. To improve predictions of environmental impact and the design of policy options for prevention, mitigation and adaptation, research plays a key role. However, to speak of "global programmes" does not seem correct to him because they are largely North-dominated, and the developing world, where 80% of children are born, is not adequately represented. He also questioned the creation of a global understanding of global problems because the scientists who represent the world's majority have difficulties with travel and communication, finances and equipment, and suffer from a lack of support and appreciation, and from isolation. Moreover, the majority of the world's states do not have their own scientific community competent to enhance the understanding of changes, causes and effects, and to inform the public as well as the politicians. Scientists can build bridges of understanding and cross barriers. But Professor Messerli estimates that under these circumstances we shall never reach political agreement about our global commons and about measures related to global change.

Sustainable development and research partnership
Sustainable development is still a very vague concept. Although many highly aggregated economic and social indicators exist, no comparable environmental indicators to evaluate environmental trends have been adopted. Chapter 40 of Agenda 21 has, therefore, stressed the need for a set of indicators of sustainable development. On the other hand we have to recognise that each country has its own priorities for data collection and analysis, reflecting local needs and circumstances. Nevertheless, Professor Messerli emphasised that we know enough to formulate an action plan at local and national levels - the dilemma is not the lack of knowledge but the conflict of interests especially within the societies of the industrialised world.

According to Professor Messerli, research partnership should consider three major issues:
- First, the challenge of narrowing the gaps between science-rich and science-poor nations. We should not believe that modern communication technologies will solve structural problems. On the contrary, the ability to transmit information cheaply and almost instantaneously does not seem to be leading to a more equitable distribution of scientific competence but is rather producing a greater concentration of it in the North.
- Second, specialisation should take entirely new forms which are problem-oriented and mostly transdisciplinary in character. The

new type of researchers understand how both natural and human social systems operate and interact, and they can think locally and globally with both a short-term and a long-term focus. In order to reach this new consciousness, key issues may only be tackled by restructuring traditional educational and research institutions and by establishing partnerships between different disciplines.
- Third, production of knowledge about the environment and development is not only a scientific issue. Traditional wisdom accumulated over generations and centuries, and informal knowledge gained from experience, often provide for sustainability better than researchers can imagine. Partnerships need to consider these domains.

"The next 30 years may be crucial"
Professor Messerli ended his introduction with a statement issued by the Royal Society of London and the US National Academy of Sciences at the Rio Conference: "If the least developed countries are forced to deal with their environmental and resource problems alone, they face overwhelming challenges". These countries have very few of the world's scientists and engineers. The next 30 years may be crucial. Therefore, Professor Messerli concluded: "we need new strategies to overcome problems in the near future. We need new partnerships for problem-oriented research, and we need this conference to think about our common responsibility".

compiled by Beat Sottas

The full texts of these contributions are available from the KFPE Secretariat

Capacity Building in Science and Technology

Keynote Address (abbreviated version) by
Mohamed H.A. Hassan *Executive Director, Third World Academy of Sciences (TWAS), Trieste, Italy*

The need for scientific capacity building in the South

Modern science and technology (S&T) have made it possible for about 20% of humanity to generate considerable wealth and enjoy a high standard of living, sharing over 85% of the world's income and contributing over 90% of the world's current scientific knowledge. But, on the other hand, the remaining 80% of humanity who inhabit three-fifths of the global village and who (for various reasons) are unable to master and utilise present day S&T are poor, deprived and marginalised. The income share of the poorest 20% is one-sixtieth of that of the richest 20%.

S&T have thus divided the global village into two parts inhabited by two distinct and highly polarised groups of people, and the gap between these two groups is widening due to:
- the rapidly advancing frontiers of modern S&T and their applications;
- the increasing cost of scientific research and the inability of poor countries to invest adequately in research and development (R&D); many of these countries, especially in Africa, are struggling with a chronic debt burden resulting in a net outflow of cash from the poor to the rich in the form of debt service;
- the declining development aid provided by the rich countries to the poor ones.

The close and intricate relationship between economic inequity and global environmental problems, both resulting from S&T, poses the greatest challenge facing humanity as it moves into the 21st century. It is only through the new forces of S&T, which have not yet been put into full action, and the collective participation of all countries, that equity and environmental sustainability can be achieved.

Problem-solving interdisciplinary research requires a very high calibre of scientists, who devote a good deal of their time to research. In most of the developing countries (DCs) scientists have very little time for research, due to heavy teaching and administrative duties and the poor working conditions which often

force them to abandon research altogether and look for additional jobs to supplement their poor salaries.
One region where capacity building is needed most is Sub-Saharan Africa, where both human resources and institutions have suffered a great deal over the past two decades as a result of natural disasters and political conflicts. Here a substantial and sustained effort to build both human and institutional capacity should be given the highest priority in the strategic agendas of governments and development co-operation agencies.

Strategies for Capacity Building
The ultimate goal of any capacity-building strategy should be to ensure the continuous availability of a minimum core of world-class scientists and technologists who, in addition to excellence in their own fields, are able to contribute effectively to national development as well as to regional and international programmes related to global issues. This calls for a new paradigm of N-S relations in which:
- development assistance to Third World countries should be largely directed towards building up, strengthening and sustaining high-level scientific and technological capacities to enable these countries to generate, manage and utilise scientific knowledge to promote sustainable economic development, and to participate fully in global environmental research;
- scientists and institutions in the N should be encouraged to work more with their counterparts in the S on problem-solving interdisciplinary research programmes. This can be greatly facilitated by modern information technologies such as electronic mail and the 'Internet' which offer immense opportunities to researchers in the S and the N to interact more effectively, exchange important data and thereby end long years of isolation and separation from each other.

The process of capacity-building varies for different countries and regions, depending on the scientific and technological level of each country in each scientific area. It is therefore necessary that a national capacity-building plan should be developed by each country and should be fully integrated into the nation's general economic development plan.

Four important factors are involved in achieving a sustainable scientific capacity: first, the capacity to develop and sustain a 'critical mass' of highly qualified scientific leadership; second, the capacity of institutions to provide adequate research facilities and attractive employment conditions; third, the capacity of scientists and institutions to contribute effectively to national development-oriented research; and finally the capacity to participate in and contribute to regional and international multi-disciplinary research programmes.

In view of this, we can broadly distinguish three capacity-building priorities for three groups of countries in the S:
- for countries with poor scientific capacity (least developed countries) priority should be given to building up and sustaining a critical mass of highly qualified scientists and to the improvement of their working conditions (salaries and research facilities);
- for countries with moderate scientific capacity (such as Colombia, Egypt, Nigeria, Pakistan, Thailand, Venezuela) priority should be given to improving the working conditions of the scientists and to involving them in development-oriented research projects;
- for countries with adequate scientific capacity (such as Argentina, Brazil, Chile, China, India, Mexico) priority should be given to improving the contacts of scientists with the outside world, and to involving them both in national development and in international research programmes.

For many African countries the priority should be to rehabilitate their universities to the highest possible level, to enable them once again to produce first-class professionals who can undertake high quality basic and applied research, and assist the national development plans of their nations. This new generation of high calibre scientists and technologists will be Africa's greatest asset and should therefore be provided with adequate working conditions so that they can devote all their time to research and teaching. The point to emphasise here is that maintaining quality should be given the highest priority in capacity-building.

Improvement in quality can also be effectively realised and sustained by setting up in the S a number of regional or international centres of excellence for postgraduate training and research, to achieve a 'critical mass' in priority areas. This should be coupled with an open competitive fellowship programme for postgraduate study and research. These centres will provide able postgraduate students with an attractive alternative to expensive study in the N and create incentives for eminent researchers to perform their work in the S. Networks of centres of excellence in

various fields of S&T should be funded and supported by governments and development co-operation agencies.
In addition to a concerted effort to build and sustain national, regional and international centres of excellence, there is a need to give exceptionally talented young scientists and outstanding individuals the encouragement and support they need to stay at home and develop their skills even when the conditions for research at their institutions are not favourable.

Discussion
Freyvogel (KFPE, Chairman Organising Committee) wanted to know about the role of both regional NGOs and the private sector within the research activities of DCs. For ***Hassan*** both are very important potential actors. The private sector might operate as an interface between science, industry and the government. However, while in industrialised countries it provides for many research activities, it is as yet nearly non-existent in DCs.
Mechkat (Module 7 project-leader, Geneva) inquired about how to integrate those representatives of local and national capacity in the S who do not surrender to the brain drain. ***Hassan*** considers this issue an extremely important one. However, a particular difficulty lies in the fact that certain capacities are often confined to small groups only and not made available to the rest of the community.
Leisinger (Ciba Geigy, Basle) had the impression that the speaker thought that research capacities should be built up in each country; he thought it wiser to spend the money where it can contribute to something specific. He pleaded for an "explicit work division in research" in order to avoid that "every country is building up capacities for everything", leading to quantity instead of quality. ***Hassan*** said that when he had declared that a national strategy, and the development of a national plan for capacity-building, should be the first priority, this did not imply there should be capacity-building in all sectors of S&T. Only those issues, fields and areas that are of high priority in a particular country need to be addressed. Nevertheless, and with regard to global concerns, he is convinced that the majority of countries need a specific capacity-building in order to address issues such as a damaged environment, poverty or sustainable development.
With regard to the mentioned negative aspects of the brain drain and the concentration of research in the N, a ***participant from***

the S wondered whether the community of researchers from the S established in the N could not be considered more positively, as an extremely mobile community able to act as an interface between N and S. He asked how we could ensure a collaboration and bridge this community gap, and how we could utilise these mobile resources as well as possible. He proposed that we should drift away from the concept of brain drain, because the globalization process - which includes scientific work too - concerns more and more the entire world, and addresses global problems. He therefore advocated a general 'brain circulation', making it possible to have scientists of excellence. *Hassan* agreed, but said we should nevertheless talk about brain drain, because the ultimate aim of training and retaining "a critical mass of highly qualified scientists and technologists available in areas of concern to the country, to the region and to the international community" must be achieved in one way or another.

Balaban addressed the problem of scientific publication and encouraged the S to take stock of its scientific literature, including both what is cited in the Science Citation Index (SCI) and Current Contents (CC) of the Institute for Scientific Information (ISI), and what is not. An existing example is that of ExtraMed, which selects the best journals from DCs for a database - mostly journals not covered either by ISI or by Medline. Both ISI and ExtraMed are private institutions which cannot cover all journals - they select the best. Balaban recommends that countries should compile their own lists of journals. A central organisation such as the African Academy of Sciences or the African Association of Science Editors could co-ordinate this effort. It might also help editors and publishers to exchange information and experience, possibly share services and initiate mergers. *Hassan* is aware of these useful programmes but thinks that scientists world-wide have a tendency to cling to the so-called international scientific publications, without caring about other locally or nationally published journals. He therefore proposed to make more efforts to include additional journals from the S in the SCI-System.

discussion compiled by Daniel Maselli

The Contribution of Research to Sustainable Development

Synthesis of the Keynote Address presented by
Uma Lele, *Advisor, Agricultural Research, Environmentally Sustainable Development, World Bank, New York*

Based on the experience of agricultural development in the Third World, Dr Lele started her presentation by stressing the central importance of agriculture and rural development to the process of economic growth in developing countries (DCs). She then outlined the importance of ensuring human and institutional development and the urgency of establishing substantial linkages in science and technology (S&T) between developed and DCs as a way of increasing agricultural productivity in a sustainable way. She pointed out that global population is growing at 100 million annually and 90 percent of that increase is taking place in DCs. Projections by the World Bank (WB) and other agencies show a growing shortage of soil and water resources in the face of this large annual population growth and an urgent need to increase productivity rapidly to keep up with the population growth. Over 60 percent of the poor live in Africa and Asia.

Lele argued that the Third World can no longer be viewed as a homogeneous entity. Southeast Asian countries have experienced rapid and broadly based economic growth led by rapid development in agriculture. The relative proportion of the population living in poverty has already declined sharply in Southeast Asia from 30 percent to 10 percent or less of the population and is projected to decline further throughout Asia during the next 20 years. Nevertheless, because Asia contains between a third and three quarters of the developing world's population, depending on where the boundaries are drawn, the absolute number of the poor in Asia will remain large, i.e. between 400 million and 500 million. Most of these future poor will be concentrated in South Asia which will contain between 250 million to 300 million of the nearly 1 billion poor people in the developing world.

In Africa, both the proportion and the absolute number of the poor are projected to increase, in no small measure due to the unsatisfactory performance of the agricultural and rural sectors.

Part III   The Contribution of Research to Sustainable Development

To increase agricultural productivity S&T must play a crucial role, together with a policy and institutional environment supportive of agriculture. Hence all kinds of scientific partnerships become very important and a number of lessons can be learnt from the successful experience of S&T partnerships which have contributed to the rapid agricultural and rural development in Asia.

Looking back to the 60s and 70s, Lele argued that agricultural research and scientific partnerships between the North and the South played a crucial role in generating the Green Revolution. The United States (US) played an important role in helping to establish a strong capacity in S&T. American scientists and scientists from the CGIAR system (cf. Keynote Touré below), which the US and WB leadership helped to establish, brought the new high yielding varieties (HYV) of wheat and rice to India. People like Norman Borlaug played a major role in that process.

Introduction of the new technology faced major opposition from virtually every corner of Indian society. Yet a handful of visionary policy-makers and scientists foresaw the potential of the HYVs and understood the vast changes in the policy, institutional, human and infrastructural changes that were required within India. These major changes were brought about within a period of 5 to 10 years. Later, as the beneficial effects of the Green Revolution became visible in increased domestic food supplies, reduced dependence on food aid and declining real food prices, others more resistant to change recognised that S&T must play an important role. This is how the necessary internal political and policy support needed for investment in agricultural research and development was created. For Lele the first Green Revolution, with all its limitations, remains an excellent example where "absolutely the best scientific know-how available at the time" was brought to bear on the most pressing hunger problem of national proportions in India. The similar spread of successful Green Revolution technology throughout Asia perhaps explains the higher standing agricultural sciences have acquired over time in many parts of Asia.

The agricultural research agenda was relatively simple in the 60s and 70s. It focused simply on increasing food production to feed the millions of people then suffering from recurring food shortages and hunger in Asia. Today's research agenda is of course much more complex. It must not only increase productivity but do so by using the minimum of modern, particularly chemical, inputs and must benefit the poor directly. The triple challenge of productivity, sustainability and poverty alleviation makes the need for S&T even more pressing, particularly in view of the highly constrained physical and financial resources in developing countries and rapidly advancing science in the industrial countries.

Lele criticised the recent excessive focus on environmental issues in the North and lamented the lack of appreciation of the equally important need to increase productivity. Today's challenge, she argued, is to bring both issues together, particularly because the global context affecting research has changed considerably. Some of the elements of the new context include:
- the competitive pressures of the more open global trading system;
- growing environmental concerns;
- the decline of official aid to DCs resulting from a combination of the end of the Cold War and "aid fatigue" in industrial countries;
- growing internal and international migration;
- the rapidly changing science in the industrial world;
- the growing role of the private sector.

As an example, privatisation of intellectual property rights in biotechnology research has created complex and as yet unresolved issues between DCs and the multinational corporations developing new technologies, with respect to access to plant genetic material of the tropics, the sharing of responsibility for it, the costs and benefits of its improvement, and particularly its availability to the poor.

The growing differentiation among DCs results in a varying ability to cope with these changes. The differences are in no small part due to major differences in the past in the investment in human and institutional capital, development policies and support for S&T in individual countries.

Those that are now the middle-income countries of Southeast Asia (e.g. Malaysia) have given greater importance to investment in S&T than have the countries in Africa. Their greater internal human and institutional capital and higher growth, in turn, places them in a stronger negotiating position for entering into partnerships with the countries of the N, e.g. in the field of biotechnology, than their poorer counterparts.

Part III The Contribution of Research to Sustainable Development

Nevertheless, even in the smallest low income African countries research capacity has increased substantially compared to the 70s and 80s. However, the financial resources at the disposal of scientists are a severe constraint in Africa. In large countries such as India shortage of funds for research is less of a real constraint, than is their efficient use! International co-operation can improve the efficiency of resource use in DCs by sharing experience of the best practices in the conduct of science.

Lele complained that universities in DCs are not being recognised sufficiently by their own governments as sources of S&T. Notwithstanding the broad differences between individual countries within Asia and Africa, there is no doubt that "Africa's problems are tremendously more complex than those of Asia". They include the small sizes of the countries, greater political instability, aid dependence, and reliance on rainfed agriculture. Unfortunately "there is no intellectual consensus on how to proceed" to address those problems. Donors do not agree with governments, or with each other. Indeed, even "within the same donor agency there is often a lack of a long-term consensus on a consistent development strategy, with changing views from day to day... Foreign aid is not only fragmented, it is uncertain, unpredictable and driven by the agenda of the donors, rather than by that of the nationals."

Externally supported investment in agricultural research in Africa provides an example. Although external assistance for agricultural development has dropped considerably in Africa, WB investments in agricultural research have increased significantly. But the proliferation of donors and the lack of consensus among them, in addition to the lack of an appropriate domestic policy environment, mentioned earlier, explains why research investments have not achieved results in terms of rapid agricultural development. Paradoxically countries which are presently doing well in agriculture (e.g. Malaysia, Indonesia, China or India) are receiving little external investment in agricultural research, perhaps because past external assistance helped to create a domestic environment able to support research, as shown in the case of India.

Lele argued that poorly administered external aid can be a substitute for the very difficult priority decisions nationals must make in allocating their own resources. The only way to improve the situation in Africa would be to develop the internal capacity to develop a lobby for agricultural research. Without internal commitment external assistance cannot have a sustainable impact. In that context SPAAR (cf. Keynote Touré below) and the CGIAR (idem) have an important role to play e.g. in fostering partnerships with national agricultural research systems (NARS) for a stronger impact.

What are the implications of this discourse for Swiss development co-operation? Lele ended by indicating - from her perspective - how Swiss aid may contribute to an improved state of affairs. She pointed out the strong commitment of Switzerland to international development and the fact that as a small and bilateral donor agency it has important advantages. In Tanzania, where she worked within the WB in the 70s and early 80s, she recalled that officials used to make a distinction between the so called 'friendly donors', who included the Dutch, the Canadians, the Swiss, the Swedes, the Norwegians, etc., and simply 'donors', such as the WB and the International Monetary Fund (IMF). She said that small bilateral donors tend to be perceived as less imposing by DCs and can therefore have stronger rapport with them. They should take advantage of that position. They should help to develop greater consensus within the donor community and foster more external investments and longer term commitments by donors, as well as strengthening relationships between institutions in the developing and the developed countries.

Furthermore, unlike the WB which is primarily a financing institution, bilateral donors have quite an important advantage. They have S&T institutions in their own countries. Bilaterals therefore must play a complementary role to multilateral donors. But Lele lamented that the internal capacity among bilateral donor agencies on development issues has declined very much in the last 20 years as they have increasingly turned to the WB for a development strategy while joining its activities by merely contributing finances. In the future very different partnerships will be needed, not just between industrialised and developing countries but among bilateral and multilateral donors, if the urgent problems which we face today are to be addressed.

Discussion

Raguram from India stressed the importance of health problems. He criticised India for the emphasis in international co-operation on sickness and illness and not on lifestyles. As an example he mentioned the battle against cancer, being fought simultaneously with the promotion of the American cigarette company ITC which is slowly managing to persuade an entire generation of Indians "that smoking is a thing you have to do". In this way, developed countries are promoting a harmful kind of lifestyle in DCs instead of promoting new kinds of international collaboration particularly in health related issues. **Lele** agreed with his concern about the adverse effects of smoking on health and the promotional role of multinationals in that respect.

An **African representative** first criticised the policy of importing certain goods from abroad without looking at the way they are being produced. He then raised the question of why - in spite of some good results from both international and national research institutions in Africa - they are "not really being used to the best advantage". One reason is probably the limited market as well as the fact that international help is "being thrown at Africa" because of the small size and the high number of countries (compared to Asia). Neighbouring countries often have the same research projects. **Lele** pointed out that a project is being carried out with the support of the SDC to look at the impact of technologies developed by international research centres in different parts of the world, in an attempt to understand why their impact is greater in some places than in others.

Alhassan (Ghana) returned to the point that Africa is not investing as much as in R&D as is Asia. His experience showed that whenever the government says there is no money, there still is money "but not for our kinds of things". It is a question of priority setting which also requires political stability. Alhassan stressed his belief in the need to change the type of training as well in order to achieve more "sandwich training".

Chiotha (Malawi) argued that donors such as the WB have a lukewarm feeling towards universities in Africa. If this really is the case, he wondered how the WB would be able to obtain the expertise it needs for research. He also pointed to the limited access to funds by researchers and universities because of the monopolisation of external funds by the governments in many African countries. This situation ought to be changed and the WB should become more aware of that problem in order to improve the situation. **Lele** replied that the low level of investment in African agriculture by the WB was in part due to a frustration about the minimal impact of past efforts in project lending, adjustment lending etc. However, she felt that there is currently greater recognition than existed 10 or 15 years ago that "development is very complicated" and that "it requires not just macropolicy reforms, nor just project lending, but a very complex blend of activities at various levels, a combination of domestic commitment and political stability". Though the challenges seem to be more complex in Africa, one way external assistance can help universities is probably by giving "intellectual respectability" to the role of universities in development and helping to provide them with a broader appeal.

Carr (USAID) wanted to know whether, while assessing the agricultural research success in Asia, Lele had developed a set of indicators allowing the success of development programmes (e.g. their sustainability) to be quantified more accurately. She also wondered whether the WB, when saying that university linkages were going to be the key to success in the agricultural research programmes, had also thought of integrating the private sector in this initiative. *Lele* explained that the factor of productivity growth has been most important for sustaining food production in Asia: "if there had been no Green Revolution in India, some 40 million more hectares of land would be needed to grow the amount of wheat consumed today". This corresponds exactly to the amount of land in the best Indian forests. She also argued that the technology which was introduced in the 60s must not be judged by today's criteria: "if we had not applied what we knew then, many many millions of people would have died". Referring to the scientific capacity developed in Asia, Lele indicated that in Pakistan, India, Bangladesh and Nepal one third of the area has now reached ceiling yield-levels. Two thirds of the area has not reached the yield ceiling. There is both a need and the potential for improvement. Finally Lele pleaded for discussions based on facts and figures rather than on emotions and stressed the importance of making better use of the information available from and about DCs.

compiled by Daniel Maselli

The Role of the World Bank

Keynote Address prepared by
Moctar Touré, *Executive Secretary Special Program for Agricultural Research SPAAR, International Bank for Reconstruction and Development (IBRD, 'World Bank'), Washington, United States*

Introduction
The World Bank (WB) was established for the reconstruction of Europe after the Second World War and to promote economic and social progress in developing nations. An important instrument in furthering progress is to expand understanding about development issues through research programs, strengthening the capacity of the Bank's clients to carry out research through credit and loan programs, establishing research partnerships with other donors and development institutions, and providing grants to other organizations to enable them to conduct research.

Bank-managed research
In the fiscal year 1994 alone, to support its portfolio the World Bank conducted 234 research projects in 9 major areas (numbers shown in brackets): Poverty and Social Welfare (28), Labor Market and Education (23), Sustainable Environmental Development (27), Infrastructure and Urban Development (13), Macroeconomics (18), International Economics (46), Domestic Finance and Capital Markets (14), Transitional Economics (39) and Private Sector Development (26).

The World Bank's research projects are funded through three channels: (i) the Bank's departments (about 50%) based on their mandate and work program, (ii) cofinancing from other agencies (about 10%) and (iii) the Central Research Support Budget (about 40%).

Special Grants Program (SGP)
Since 1973 the Bank has supported and allocated funds to the SGP as an important development instrument. The SGP is intended to support research and development programs that address significant global or regional development issues which are not suitable for Bank loans or IDA credits, and do not fit into the Bank's country-focused operational programs. Support is often

targeted towards regional or global initiatives involving special skills and institutional arrangements outside the Bank. The SGP usually funds projects in collaboration with other donors and the beneficiary countries.

Some of the SGP programs are collaborative, and are overseen and coordinated by the Bank. It also contributes to collaborative programs promoted by other agencies. Such programs have been in the fields of development of agricultural technology, eradication or control of tropical diseases, institution-building, training of researchers, and support for non-governmental organizations (NGOs) and other institutions concerned with knowledge-based development issues.

Consultative Group on International Agricultural Research (CGIAR)

The CGIAR is an informal association of public and private sector donors, who support a network of 16 international agricultural research centers. The group was established in 1971. It was co-sponsored by the Food and Agriculture Organization (FAO), The World Bank, the United Nations Development Program (UNDP), and the United Nations Environmental Program (UNEP). At the beginning it was dominated by the North; however, in recent years about 14 developing countries (DCs) have joined the group as donors (CGIAR, 1995). The Bank hosts the Secretariat of the CGIAR, provides the chairmanship, and contributes to the funding of the CGIAR system as a donor of last resort. This funding is channeled through the SGP.

The international centers in the CGIAR system are part of a global agricultural research system. They carry out six categories of research (CGIAR 1995): (i) Productivity Research; (ii) Management of Natural Resources; (iii) Improving the Policy Environment i.e. assisting DCs to formulate and carry out effective food, agriculture, and research policies; (iv) Institution Building i.e. strengthening national agricultural research systems (NARSs) in DCs; (v) Germplasm Conservation i.e. conserving germplasm and making it available to all regions and countries; (vi) Building Linkages i.e. facilitating co-operation between advanced institutions in DCs and national research programs in DCs.

The production and the productivity of CGIAR-mandated crops in DCs has increased considerably between 1970 and 1994 due to an increase in yield and area planted.

Despite its success, in 1994 the CGIAR system was facing a decline in funding that threatened the implementation of research programs in the centers. This forced the CGIAR to launch a renewal program in which the World Bank provided the needed leadership. The Bank offered to match in 1994 and 1995 additional contributions from other CGIAR members to raise the estimated level of funding. This offer was reciprocated by several members, and in 1994 funding rose by $48 million from the original estimate of $215 million. In addition, the renewal program brought about changes by clarifying the vision of the system, re-focusing its agenda, creating greater openness and transparency, strengthening its partnerships, ensuring its effectiveness and efficiency, and improving its governance and operations.

Special Program for African Agricultural Research (SPAAR)
Included in the international agricultural research allocation of the SGP is the Bank's contribution to the budget of the Special Program for African Agricultural Research (SPAAR). SPAAR was established in 1985 when donors were concerned about the inadequate impact of technology in Sub-Saharan Africa (SSA). The program was convened as an informal mechanism to improve donor consultation and collaboration with the objective of stimulating and sustaining the capacities of the national agricultural research systems (NARS) in SSA.

During the 10th Plenary in May 1990, SPAAR donors adopted a more pro-active agenda based on regional Frameworks for Action (FFAs). The FFAs, which are currently at the core of SPAAR's program and mandate, provide the scope, orientation, and guidelines to strengthen NARS within a regional context. The FFAs seek to revitalize agricultural research through institutionalizing a strategic planning process that is participatory and responsive; developing sustainable funding mechanisms; improving institutional management and creating transparency and accountability; building country coalitions and support groups that involve all the stakeholders; strengthening links between researchers, extension services, farmers and markets, and promoting regional and international collaboration to ensure cost effectiveness and spillover effects.

In 1990 SPAAR members agreed to support existing regional research organizations, in Southern Africa the Southern Africa Center for Co-operation in Research and Training (SACCAR), and in the Sahel the Institut du Sahel (INSAH), and also to prepare a research strategy for the SSA sub-regions that did not yet have regional research organizations. Tanzania and Mali were selected as the pilot countries to implement the FFA principles in Southern Africa and the Sahel. By 1995 four regional FFAs had been developed: for Southern Africa, the Sahel, Eastern and Central Africa, and the Humid and Sub-Humid zones of West and Central Africa. A new regional collaborative mechanism was created: the Association for Strengthening Agricultural Research in Eastern and Central Africa (ASARECA). In West and Central Africa the FFA process led to the transformation of the 'Conférence des Résponsables de Recherche Agronomique Africains' (CORAF) into a fully-fledged regional coordinating body. NARS leaders in the region also decided to merge the FFAs of the Sahel and the Humid and Sub Humid zones.

The WB hosts SPAAR's small secretariat as well as providing the chairmanship. It has also incorporated some of the FFA principles into agricultural research projects funded through the Bank's loans and IDA credits. In addition, the Bank contributed about 28.7% of the funding of SPAAR's Business Plan in 1996, i.e., about $0.876 million, to support its objectives, which are (i) to support the implementation of the FFA principles in selected SSA countries and sub-regions; (ii) to establish or strengthen sub-regional collaborative mechanisms and a SSA forum for agricultural research; and (iii) to provide support services for coalition building/linkages with donors as well as between research, extension services and end-users of technology.

SGP in health, education and environment
The Bank also funds research in health (tropical diseases, human reproduction, safe motherhood, child survival, AIDS, population nutrition, river blindness). In education, the bank supports several projects through the SGP; namely: the Africa Capacity Building Initiative, Donors to African Education, McNamara Fellowships, and Education for All. On environmental issues the Bank, through SGP, supports projects such as the Mediterranean Environment Technical Assistance Program and the Danube Program. Additional environmental projects are also supported through the Global Environmental Facility (GEF). Small contributions are also made in the areas of urban development, infrastructure, and private sector development.

World Bank's research portfolio
The World Bank supports research projects in its member countries through projects financed by IBRD loans and IDA credits. A review of the Bank's agricultural portfolio illustrates the role it plays in supporting research in general. This portfolio consists of free standing agricultural research projects (FSARP), in which research is the primary objective, and projects in agricultural and rural development (ARD) that contain at least one research component.
In 1994, about 185 projects (25 FSARP and 160 non-FSARP) contained at least one agricultural research component. These projects had a total cost of $20.2 billion: $1.7 billion for FSARP and $18.5 billion for non-FSARP with research components. However, of the total of $20.2 billion, only about $2.2 billion, or 10.9%, was specifically earmarked for agricultural research ($1.3 billion for FSARP and $0.9 billion for non-FSARP). The share of research projects of the costs of the total agricultural portfolio (including projects with no research components), was 26%, of which 2% were FSARP and 24% were non-FSARP.
A comparison of the WB's portfolio for the Fiscal Years 1981-87 and 1988-94 shows a decrease of 20% for agricultural research operations from 230 to 185 projects, representing a 13% decrease in project costs. This was associated with a decrease in the number of agricultural operations from 467 to 371 for the same period. However, total actual expenditure on agricultural research increased from $1.5 billion in 1981-87 to $2.2 billion for 1988-94.

Regional allocation of research expenditure
The distribution of research expenditure across the regions is as follows: Sub-Saharan Africa (SSA) received the largest share, $1.0 billion (46%). South Asia (SAS) received $473 million (21%), Latin America and the Caribbean (LAC) received $407 million (18%), the Middle East and North Africa (MNA) received $165 million (7%), East Asia and the Pacific (EAP) received $126 million (6%), and Europe and Central Asia (ECA) $29.8 million (1%). This trend reflects the need for strengthening agricultural research in these regions as well as the importance of agriculture in the economies of these regions (cf. relationship between agricultural and research portfolios).

Dissemination of research findings
Numerous publications result from research managed by the Bank's departments, the SGP and the Bank's research portfolio. This information is widely disseminated through libraries, the Bank's bookstore, and its Resident Missions in member countries. The Bank, the recipients of SGP and its clients also carry out extensive training programs to enhance the capacity for research in all socioeconomic fields.

Text adapted by Daniel Maselli from a paper prepared by Moctar Touré but not presented at the Conference

The Private Sector and Research Partnership

Keynote Address by
Michael Kohn, *Chairman of the Institute for "Capital and Economy",*
Zurich

The need for international collaboration and the role of science
The past three decades have witnessed a *tremendous economic and technological change in the developing world.* Fundamental to this transformation has been *the large-scale importation of technology from industrialised nations*, for establishing the infrastructure essential for industrialisation and other forms of economic development.
However, to cope with the enormous global problems facing us today, *trade and technology transfer is not sufficient*. Partnership in the field of science and development can make a valuable contribution to addressing global problems.
In parallel with the rapid importation by developing countries (DCs) of sophisticated technology-based infrastructure systems, considerable efforts should be made to establish, develop and diversify their basic science and technology capabilities. 'Rio' has proved that the situation of research and science in DCs is indeed alarming. The South largely depends on results from research done in the industrialised countries.
In the last years the general attitude and understanding of the need to promote N-S partnership in science has made progress. Many universities and research institutes around the world have started to look more actively into this matter and various institutes of technology have started to provide developing and newly industrialised nations with improved access to the scientific and technological capabilities of the industrialised world. But in spite of this, *collaborative research is not (or not yet) on the agenda. Downstream operations are in order, but upstream operations are not, or not yet.*
Why is co-operation in the field of Research and Development (R&D) still lagging behind and why is it not up to the expectations of the scientific community, although some progress can be detected? The following list - which is not exhaustive - attempts to give a first answer on the level of the micro-economy, reflecting the attitudes and motives of single enterprises, be they private or public.

The braking forces in the implementation of collaborative research with the Third World

❶ Science is the top not the bottom
International suppliers maintain that to build up a position in, or a relation with a country, first local business, local manufacturing, and a local office are needed. From the point of view of the export industry in the N, R&D are the crown of the matter, not the beginning!

❷ Utility first
Collaborative research in the eyes of industry is welcome only if it leads to success and this is also true for scientific activities. What industrial firms aim at is in-house research first, and when it comes to collaboration with a partner, even in the Western world, the guiding principle is utility.

❸ Question of language
Since verbal communication can facilitate understanding or render it more difficult, different languages can be a major hindrance.

❹ Concentration on emerging markets
Scientific activities are part of a company's overall marketing and business strategy. The Swiss economy concentrates business on countries of the OECD and on countries in transition. In addition, countries with emerging markets, like some in Asia, are given more attention than the least developed countries (LDCs), also in respect to scientific co-operation. *The guiding rule of business is maintaining or increasing the market share.*

❺ Lower level of education and scientific standing
The lower level of education, the lower scientific standing and the missing technical tradition in the S have negative repercussions on the readiness of business and industry of the N to enter joint research projects with DCs and LDCs. The fact that, rightly or wrongly, *the scientist of the developed world does not consider his colleague from the S as equal partner*, has or has had an impeding impact on N-S research programs.

❻ "Brain drain" of qualified scientists to other occupations
The lack of a clear research policy in many DCs does not make it inviting to consider continuous collaborative research. To achieve real and lasting solutions of our global problems, the critical situation of scientific research in the DCs must improve drastically. They must be willing and must be enabled to approach their problems autonomously and independently. It is also very much in the interest of the N that the DCs should increase their capacities for problem solving.

❼ Research and development needs money
The crucial problem in connection with research activities in general is the tightness of budgets. National budget deficits and lack of financial means in the many branches of industry have induced many research institutes to cut expenditure. This applies not only to the private sector but even more to the public sector.

❽ Financial squeeze for foreign aid programs
The funding of foreign aid is undergoing a severe squeeze in many if not in all Western countries. Nevertheless, it is the strong will of the Swiss Government to reach the planned Swiss target of 0.4% of the GNP to be invested in the N-S co-operation. However, it frequently happens that the parliament curtails such plans.

❾ The appetite for high technology
DCs often wish to practise research in the spheres of high technology, while it would be more beneficial for them to be provided with items and solutions which are robust, solid, simple and easy to handle. There is a tendency in the Third World to ask for technical installations, power plants, chemical plants etc. which are so sophisticated that an engineer or technician with an average education cannot grasp them. Yet the blame should not only be put on the demanding client in Africa or Asia, but also on the business-minded supplier in Europe or the USA, who has a commercial interest in selling sophisticated solutions.

❿ Uncertainty about political and economic stability
Although it is not mentioned openly, it can be felt in the course of discussions that there is still a lack of confidence about whether contractual obligations will be kept. The partner from the N would like to see favourable framework conditions like political stability, commercial credit-worthiness, an equitable return on investment, free transfer of profits abroad, protection of patents and a favourable climate for foreign investors.

This list of 10 impediments, leading to a lack of enthusiasm for entering long-term N-S collaborative projects, is not exhaustive. Maybe some of the reasons are exaggerated and only an alibi for non-action - but for whatever reason, the non-action is there. However, the list should not be demotivating. What is important is *the mutual understanding that collaborative research can only be successful when the economy and the industry are involved* - and the more the world economy is flourishing, the better is the chance for R&D. It should not be forgotten that "Sustainable Development" rests on three pillars: ecology, social welfare and the economy - very often the economy is forgotten...

"Eppur si muove" - nevertheless there is progress

In spite of the many hurdles on the way to collaborative research things are moving. In Switzerland, there are already several institutions geared to development education and research collaboration, and there are institutions abroad which were originally Swiss foundations and are still strongly supported by Switzerland. It seems as if the scientific community in the western world has begun to understand the message. For example the Massachusetts Institute of Technology (MIT) already set up a Technology and Development Program (TDP) in 1971 in order to provide developing and newly-industrialised nations with improved access to the scientific and technological capabilities of the industrialised world.

Swiss scientific institutions cannot show a similar record, but nevertheless in Switzerland things are moving, too - a bit slowly, but thoroughly. Asea Brown Boveri (ABB) has entered a scientific collaboration with the Tsinghua University in Bejing on "Clean and Efficient Utilisation of Coal". The Paul Scherrer Institute (PSI) has engaged itself in different projects under the umbrella of scientific partnership, e.g. on solar-thermal power for DCs and on decomposition of limestone in a solar reactor. The institute is inviting postdoctoral students from the S to work there for a period, and has joined the Alliance for Global Sustainability concerned with transport technology, sustainable mobility and other problems of cities. There is no doubt that other Swiss industrial firms and research institutes have started to co-operate with the S.

"Help yourself - the doors are open"

The N is and must be interested in scientific co-operation with the rest of the world. But it is also a must that DCs address the problems themselves. The present scientific community in the world is open. Everyone can enter the door if he/she demonstrates know-how and performance. Science nowadays is an open book. Scientific data is accessible for everybody. "Free-riding" has no perspective in the world of research. Thus it is indispensable that the Third World promotes its own scientific education (like, for example, Taiwan).

Parallel to the endeavours of the DCs themselves, the industrialised world will have to back up the efforts of the S with financial and human capital. The more we all become aware that the world is a global village, the more we will recognise that R&D is a part of it.

text abbreviated by Daniel Maselli

Discussion

For **Jain** (Delhi University, India) motivation is an essential factor in partnership. Hence commercial establishments (and academic institutions, too) do not support research collaboration for purely philanthropic motives but mainly for their own commercial interests. There is competition among and between national and multinational organisations in the field of research, and also industrial spying; both appear to be serious hindrances for research partnerships within the private sector. Furthermore the agendas of multinational donor organisations are often influenced by their financial supporters and do not therefore address the issues which concern the local population. Jain also indicated that companies often leave their home country because, for example, of severe environmental or bureaucratic burdens, and continue producing in a DC without worrying about ecological, social and other consequences of their activity.

Kohn agreed with most of Jain's statements but refuted the suggestion that northern companies would not apply the same high standards with respect e.g. to the environment in DCs as they do in their home countries. While this might have been the case for a while, more and more multinationals are applying the same technology and technique in DCs as they do at home. There are two main reasons for that: 1) sooner or later the prescriptions for environmental protection will improve in these countries, and it will be more expensive to adapt than to start with the 'best'; 2) an international or multinational company profits from having the same technology all over the world (e.g. for controlling, replacements, renewals etc.).

Thereafter two other questions were raised from the *floor*: 1) Is there anything that S-S collaboration can learn from N-N collaboration experience? 2) Is it easier for strong institutions (N) to build partnerships than it is for the weak ones (S) who depend upon collaboration in order to strengthen themselves? **Kohn** said that the N is learning from such collaborations, too, and that the globalisation of problems is forcing everybody to work across borders, so that science and research must become more international. This globalisation has an impact on co-operation. High performance, high skill and strong commitment are important: "The brains that people have got from God are the same for all of us: it's the framework conditions that have to be changed so that we all can collaborate on the same level".

Another **participant from the S** pointed out that industry in the western world is getting larger and more capital intensive while most DCs would like to have smaller, labour intensive industries in rural areas. He suggested aiming at a different kind of industrial development, with something small for rural areas and something labour-intensive for urban areas. **Kohn** agreed that the 'megathinking' of the N cannot be applied to the S - though experience has shown that whenever the DCs ask for megasolutions the N delivers them.

Again a *participant from the S* reminded the Conference that the private sector in the N is spending much more money on research than the public sector (Panel) and that it is largely export-oriented, which means that part of this research in the N is being done for products to be sold in the S. Would it not be justifiable to request the private sector in the N to invest more in research in the S and to involve local capabilities in order to solve the South's problems? **Kohn** pointed out that most of Switzerland's exports go to European countries. Nevertheless he agreed that in fact industry in the N is directed strongly towards emerging markets such as Asia, causing important changes. However, he worries less about such countries, than about LDCs which have no real market potential and might be left aside. Of course the expectations of countries with an emerging market will generate big problems, too. For example, in China, hundreds of millions of cars are to be produced, while the global CO_2 problem is endangering life on earth. **Thierstein** (Chairman) reminded the Conference that through the SPPE-Module 7 a better understanding of the problems in the S is being generated, which should help us to address these problems better in the future.

Another *participant* contested the "open door statement" saying it was a "very rosy picture". While in some places doors may open (e.g. in Eastern Europe) in other places they may close (e.g. in Africa). **Kohn** replied that what he intended to say was that there is an improved access to scientific information, contacts etc. in a more open world. The DCs should therefore become more active themselves in order to solve some problems on their own. "Once you have entered the open doors, you will start opening the closed ones from the inside."

compiled by Daniel Maselli

Part III   Contributions to the Conference

Concepts of Research Partnership
Summary of the Round Table

Rolf Carlmann, Director, Department for Research Cooperation,
SAREC-SIDA, Stockholm (Sweden)

Teresa Fogelberg, Head, Research Programme, Directorate for
General Development Cooperation (DGIS), The Hague (Netherlands)

Martin Khor, Research Director, Consumers' Association of Penang,
Pulau Pinang (Malaysia)

Bakary Ouayogodé, Research Director, Dept. of Education and
Scientific Research, Abidjan (Ivory Coast)

Moderator: *Rolf Probala*, Head, News Department, Swiss Broadcasting Corporation, Zurich

The Round Table discussion aimed at comparing concepts of research partnership currently in use in countries or organisations which have considerable experience in this domain. In order to obtain a broad range of standpoints reflecting different priorities, the conveners of the Conference invited representatives from the North and South as well as from government agencies and from NGOs to explain and discuss their concepts. As well as the established patterns, this Round Table talk also offered the opportunity of outlining some desirable changes or alternative models.

The prevailing partnerships are often characterised by a setting in which a Northern researcher or research organisation has to deal with money which has been allocated to a project by a donor or a research funding agency. According to **Rolf Carlmann,** director of the department for research cooperation of the official Swedish agency for development cooperation (SAREC-SIDA), donors have, therefore, a great opportunity to influence the imbalances and to define the extent to which the Southern partner has control over the budget. Instead of subordinating Southern partners, it is possible to advocate shared or even equal responsibility for budgeting and reporting, as well as for publication activities, training and the dissemination of results.

An alternative to the prevailing bilateral partnership is the consortium approach. It is based on strategic cooperation between interested groups on both sides, the donors and the researchers.

Part III   Round Table: Concepts of Research Partnership

Rolf Carlmann wanted first to clarify expressions such as Third World or the South. According to him, such generalisations are becoming meaningless. These categories in fact describe a very heterogeneous range of countries in different stages of development and with different needs, priorities and potential. The efforts of Sweden mainly aim at empowering the poorer developing countries with a weak research base. Given this premise, capacity-building is indeed the main objective. The Swedish approach emphasises cooperation between universities and research training, whereby the recipients remain in their home countries with only short periods based in Sweden. Capacity-building is further strengthened by support for overhead costs, e.g. research management, infrastructure, libraries, laboratories etc. In any case it is important that the collaboration is an intellectual exercise which is not donor-driven. Because universities are the heart of research, Sweden aims at supporting them over a very long period. This approach is meant to prevent the inadequacies and pitfalls of the project approach. According to Mr. Carlmann, this approach tends to focus on short term issues and immediate applicability. There is a tendency to chase researchers and to fragment the endeavour, so that institution and capacity-building is neglected.

Bakary Ouayogodé, research director at the Department of Education and Scientific Research of the Ivory Coast, emphasised that research partnerships have to enhance social and economic development. In practice, this implies three key concepts:
1) most crucial is an appropriate understanding of the end-user, be it farming communities or women or other targeted categories;
2) the notion of equity and equality requires the sharing of means and benefits as well as a definition of the research agendas in collaboration with the poor;
3) although this is highly problematic, research partnerships should address daily life issues and basic needs. Accordingly, research has to push small, cost-effective technologies and to stress training and education.
A developing country also has to stress partnership in order to overcome fragmentation between research institutions and universities. Another important issue is the willingness and involvement of governments and political leaders from developing countries. Up to now, they have often been reluctant, but they have to come up with support for their own researchers in order to develop the potential for equitable partnerships.

Part III Round Table: Concepts of Research Partnership

Teresa Fogelberg from the Directorate for General Development Cooperation of the Netherlands suggested that research partnership has first to tackle the problem of asymmetry. Recent shifts in Dutch policy, therefore, aim at counterbalancing the prevailing patterns; the premises are ownership by the recipients, demand orientation, and capacity-building so that Southern researchers and institutions are empowered to play a full role in the research arena. Ideally, this requires long-term financial support for 10 to 15 years to multidisciplinary teams or networks, without imposing specific agendas. Moreover, it is very important to decrease dependency on one donor. Radical attempts at partnerships should consider handing over budgetary responsibilities to Southern partners, or having a majority of members from developing countries in the steering committee.

In line with these arguments, **Martin Khor** from the Penang Consumers' Association, an important non-governmental research agency, advocated a change of perspective and orientation which would allow the serious crisis in both development and research to be faced. Most of the uncertainty is caused by the tremendous impact of economic and social processes at global level (IMF, World Bank, WTO/ TRIPS related issues of intellectual property and patents) where the governments from the South - not to speak of the farmers or other rather remote knowledge-owners - do not really have negotiating power. In order to create awareness among the people and the policy makers, Khor stated that the South needs capacity-building. However, he suggested that one has to look not only at universities and formal scientific systems, but also at informal and non-governmental systems. At present, local movements which focus on one issue have started to build research capabilities. From such a position it is possible to lobby at government level and to influence decision-making with respect to national policies. However, some independent NGOs engaged in research have gone one step further and initiated networking at a global level (Third World Network). This kind of partnership allows for a comprehensive monitoring of social, economic and environmental issues. The advisory capacities so derived strengthen the position of the organisations concerned: they can lobby or press for changes, but they can also advise their governments as to what kind of negotiating position they could be taking in international talks.

The discussion of a series of issues and/or questions raised by members of the audience revealed that the concepts of partnership presented did not in fact address some sensitive issues. In particular, participants from the South questioned representatives from the

North about underlying concepts, hidden agendas and action plans regarding changes of prevailing asymmetries and inequalities.

Lotfia el Nadi from Cairo University and Qatar University pointed to the fact that partnership also means to assess and to classify needs. Cases of countries with no idea of how to start were rare; many countries know what they want for development but lack money or capacity. Concepts of partnership could be defined according to this typology, and the extent of support needed for take-off identified.

K. Balasubramanian from the Swaminathan Foundation in New Delhi stated that conditions for partnership have worsened. Mutual trust and mutual benefit have been sacrificed in recent years, and a nonsensical attitude is being imposed by international organisations such as the WTO and the TRIPS regulations it imposed: knowledge has now become a commodity on the global market. He urged the audience to think about the ethics which must be developed in such settings of unequal and coercive partnerships.

Oumar Niangado, director of the Institute of Rural Economy in Mali, wanted to place research partnerships in the context of the current financial crisis and the crisis of confidence. Whereas the effects of the former are obvious, one should not forget that local people are now disappointed, and farmers who have the potential for change now seek independent routes, e.g. through NGOs. Both lead to a situation which weakens the position of Southern partners and increases their dependence on donors in the North.

Before going into a discussion of concepts of partnership, **Deon Carstens** from South Africa reminded the audience that there is harsh competition between competencies and capacities in the South and the North, and the former are not given room for development.

Lorenzo Zolezzi from the Law faculty of a Peruvian university got the impression that this Round Table still reflected the same positions defended in the great discussions of the seventies about partnerships in the social sciences. Although some spectacular results had been produced in the short term, Southern concepts had no chance because international organisations imposed some subjects of their own preference, e.g. women's rights, ecology and sustainability, good governance etc. Local researchers and organisations need capacity-building which enables them to cope with the internationally set agendas.

Khotso Mokhele from South Africa agreed with Dr. Fogelberg's statement about asymmetries. Therefore, he emphasised, ethics must underpin the partnerships. Since the North has an agenda of its own which has worked well for a century, the South has to take responsibility and to generate its own research proposals. Moreover, the intellectual resources available have to be injected into the projects so that collaborative efforts can withstand the asymmetries.

When talking about new concepts of partnership **Isabelle Milbert** rejected the optimistic view of Martin Khor about the potential of NGOs. She reminded the audience that they are often in a weak position due to their modalities of action, and their capabilities may not match those of international research. They lack the ability both for dialogue and for dissemination.

In their closing remarks, the participants of the Round Table emphasised some of the crucial aspects of any partnership concept. **Rolf Carlmann** pointed at the fact that capacity-building, which is crucial, has to be goal-related and context-related. **Bakary Ouayogodé** on the other hand, had a less utilitarian view: partnerships of any kind are a must to tackle shortage of financial means, to compensate for losses due to brain drain, and to tap the mainstreams of information and knowledge. However, according to him, the necessarily stronger donor partner should be led by a little humanitarian understanding and, therefore, respect ethics and honesty. **Teresa Fogelberg** agreed with this suggestion but warned against understanding the concept of partnership either as a romantic alliance or a marriage of convenience. Given the pressure of a globalised economy she thought that competition between research institutions was sound. However, full individual responsibility and sustainable cooperation can only be achieved when conditions, agendas and steps are spelled out. **Martin Khor** advocated a flexible concept of partnership. Referring to a proposal of the Swiss strategy he advised the audience to avoid rigid definitions and other formal criteria, like having an equal number of scientists from both North and South. There is a large number of more innovative models emanating either from centres in the South or universities or donors in the North. As for the crucial point of capacity-building he claims that this has to happen not only in oriented research but also in research management, conceptualisation and leadership.

compiled by Beat Sottas

International Competition for Research in the South - International Programmes and the Experiences of Different Partners

Summary of the Panel Discussion

Participants
Christian Bonte-Friedheim, *Director General, International Service for National Agricultural Research (ISNAR), The Hague, The Netherlands*
Jacques Charmes, *Head, Department of Societies, Urbanisation and Development at the French Scientific Research Institute for Development and Co-operation (ORSTOM), Paris, France*
Rolf Korte, *Head, Department of Health, Population and Nutrition at the Deutsche Gesellschaft für technische Zusammenarbeit (GTZ), Eschborn, Germany*
Hugo Romero, *Head, Graduate School, School of Architecture and Urbanism, University of Chile, Santiago, Chile*
Leena Srivastava, *TATA Research Institute, New Delhi, India*

Moderator
John Howell, *Director, Overseas Development Institute (ODI), London, United Kingdom*

Confronting three representatives from European countries (France, Germany and The Netherlands) responsible for scientific research in developing countries (DCs) with two active researchers from the S (Chile and India; *George Benneh*, Vice-Chancellor of the University of Ghana, sent last-minute regrets), the Panel Discussion opened the second day of the Conference by addressing the issue of international scientific competition.
Howell perceived four different kinds of competitive fields: competition among Northern research institutes, competition between Northern and Southern institutes for resources and ownership of research, competition among Northern institutes for Southern partners, and - last but not least - competition among

Southern institutes themselves. He encouraged the participants to present their analysis of the "research market and possible market imperfections" as well as their programmes and the lessons learned from their own work.

He compared the different countries represented and characterised Chile as a "middle income country, with a well developed research capacity, perfectly capable of developing its own research partnerships without the need for external support", India as a "low income country" but with a "very substantial research capacity" and "one of the leading research countries in the South", where the "direction of aid for research is in the hands of the Indian government and institutions" and therefore capable of setting "their own terms for any external collaboration". He regretted the absence of the invited representative from Ghana, also a "low income country" but unlike India suffering from weak research structures, an "unsupportive policy environment" and strongly dominant external financing which "makes Ghana highly vulnerable to external dictation of its research".

Regarding the three representatives of the N, Howell pointed out the different characteristics of their organisations. ISNAR is an international organisation with an explicit mandate to strengthen research institutions, particularly in agriculture, GTZ and ORSTOM are both national organisations more or less linked to their governments, while ODI, as an independent economic research institute without a core programme, gets no such support.

Romero described the paradigm of the recent development of Chile, where a successful political transition and economic growth (7%/y) causes not only difficulties in allocating funds for aid and research but also tremendous environmental damage and increasing social disparities. In fact the Chilean success story is based on careless exploitation of natural national resources: 50% of all national income comes from the strongly supported mining industry. The exploitation of the Atacama Desert consumes 7'000 litres of water per second, causing enormous environmental stress. There are similar problems with fishing, forestry and agriculture. While the richest 20% of the population receive nearly 50% of the national income, the poorest 10% get less than 3%. To avoid a major collapse Chile has to develop regulations and strategies in domains of major concern like the environment, social issues, and the development of the economy. This requires the help of scientific research but "because of the rapid economic growth, the population is not much interested in research any more". Chile does have nearly 70 universities, but these have become a business since they are not doing research, but are mostly preparing professionals for the private sector - despite being supported by public funds. Although the private sector controls more than 80% of the economy, it invests almost no money in research.

"One main difference between developed and undeveloped countries is probably the fact that most of our decisions are not taken on a basis of scientific knowledge and facts." (Romero)

Romero advocated collaborative processes, e.g. between the government and the scientific community, between the private and public sectors, or with other "middle class countries", rather than competition. As long as the research done by the N mainly aims at publishing articles in internationally respected journals, such competition will make no sense because the needs of local people are not being addressed. Instead, decision-makers should be provided with useful information as well as scientific knowledge, and the results diffused locally to the people directly concerned. Therefore more applied research able to address real critical issues, like the water problem of the Atacama, ought to be undertaken. Partnerships should make use of the capacities of both N and S: sophisticated equipment and research techniques on one side, databases and the familiarity with the local reality as well as the ability to communicate the results to the authorities and to local people, on the other.

Howell summarised Romero's last points as "domestic competition for research resources and priorities, where the areas of natural resources depletion and the area of economic policies that would promote growth with social justice and income distribution are losing badly".

Srivastava explained that for the TATA Energy Research Institute the search for funding is crucial (there is no regular support either from the government or from industrial conglomerates). Proposals either fit the guidelines of a funding organisation or a lot of time and energy is needed to find a donor organisation whose funding priorities or guidelines match the projects submitted. Experience has shown that priorities set by the donors are (a) often very similar, and (b) related to areas of actual current concern. This means that not (yet) fashionable topics (as environmental issues were 15 years ago in India) will rarely be supported. Donors should therefore not only react to a crisis on a short term basis, but consider potential longer term concerns too. The currently ongoing processes of economic reform in India are a recent example: while the energy sector is particularly concerned about meeting energy demand and activities are being undertaken to promote or bring in the private sector, not enough attention is being paid to the implications of such reforms on the social fabric of the economy (cf. Romero). To avoid this, the foreign donor organisations active in a country should co-ordinate their programmes, thus allowing less glamorous topics which are nevertheless important to be addressed. In fact two main kinds of research donors seem to be emerging in India:

a) Bilaterally operating agencies, traditionally focusing primarily on development and action programmes, where the little research conducted is/was mostly done by their own nationals. The relatively new concept of research partnership has been promoted by some changes in attitude and by lessons learnt. The N increasingly recognises the local technical capabilities of the S, but the application of research know-how from the N in the S is not that easy. The S shows an increasing unhappiness with the traditional models of international assistance. Globalisation is increasing rapidly, also raising the need for more R&D funds, and finally, budgets are simultaneously being cut and greater accountability for the research is being required.

"At least in some countries of the world aid contributions are being used directly or indirectly to create or to continue employment opportunities in the North." (Srivastava)

b) Multilateral organisations from the corporate world. The opening of the Indian economy has created enormous interest within many multinational organisations involved in development; they increasingly recognise the capacities existing in some countries of the S though many of them have programmes which serve their own industry and service sectors first! Fortunately the pressure to involve local experts, in bi- as well as multilateral organisations, is growing.

Srivastava also criticised the way that too often important international organisations (e.g. the World Bank) are headed by people from the N. Consequently their concerns are being taken into consideration more than those of representatives from the S.

Howell commented on two facts: 1) bilateral donors are often subject to commercial and industrial pressures; 2) political imperatives often guide the direction of research aid, setting priorities. Emphasising that the Indian research community is well placed to identify those different pressures and resist them he again pointed towards Ghana, which has more or less surrendered its research programme to the competing demands of external donors.
"Research partnership is a cloak for research direction from the North." (Howell)

Bonte-Friedheim first compared the characteristics of partners. The Netherlands has about 150'000 farmers; each inhabitant has theoretically about 0.06 hectare of agricultural land. This is about the same as the Swiss and Japanese have, but also about the same as a Bangladeshi or Egyptian. The farmers in The Netherlands produce about 4% of the GNP while 500 million USD are being spent on agricultural research. This is about the same as the expenditures of all countries of sub-Saharan Africa on agricultural research. France spends about 2 billion USD on agricultural research, which is about the same as the total that all DCs spend on research in that domain. Bonte-Friedheim then pleaded for a clear distinction between *capacity-building*, which is human resource development, and is negatively affected by the "brain drain", and *institution-building and strengthening*. In many countries, especially in Africa, this has become the number one concern, and is affected by "brain waste". The problems and causes related to that are: little priority setting in monitoring and evaluation, weak linkages to external services e.g. to the farmers and to the universities inside and outside the country, limited access to knowledge, imbalance in the disciplines, weak governance and weak political support, very little research funding available (since most of the funds go for salaries, "researchers have a pencil and that is about all"). The result of this is that the best people go to industry and most of the institutions become unsustainable.

"Good scientists are becoming research managers without being trained for it - that's a brain waste because they are not doing what they are trained for and are good at." (Bonte-Friedheim)

With regard to the special situation of agricultural research it seems to be widely assumed that there is only one type of research and very little competition between the different actors. One has to distinguish between basic, strategic, applied, and adaptive research, as well as demonstrations. There are special advanced research institutions, mainly in DCs, concentrating their activities on so-called upstream research. There are the national agricultural research systems (NARS) and the industry in the DCs, which undertake adaptive, applied and some strategic research. Finally, there are the farmers and the NGOs which concentrate on demonstrations and undertake a limited amount of adaptive research. In many DCs, testing and demonstrations in the field of agriculture are certainly part of research.

Government expenditure on agricultural research as a percentage of the country's agricultural gross national product (AgGNP) varies widely. In low-income countries it is about 0.5%, in middle-income countries over 2%, and in high-income countries it can be as much as 4% or 5%. Unfortunately, the growth rates in agricultural research expenditure in African NARS have declined during the last three decades, from 6% in the 1960s to more than 2.5% in the 1970s, to virtually no growth in the last 10-15 years. At the same time, the number of research staff has increased significantly. As a result the expenditure per researcher has decreased during the last 30 years, whereas in many developed countries the funds available for each researcher have gone up. Of course this situation varies widely all over the world.

While past partnerships were mainly supply-driven, aid-tied and often serving the goals of those who provided the aid, future ones should be demand-driven and based on national priorities "putting relevance first and maybe quality second." Finally, Bonte-Friedheim proposed that research institutions in the N and in the S should use modern information technologies to set up a kind of "stock exchange". It must be clearly stated what is wanted and needed and what is offered and available. The results of such partnerships will be fewer disappointments and fewer links based on relationships between individual scientists.

"The search for the best is the worst enemy of the good." (Bonte-Friedheim)

Korte first pointed to a problem caused by the N: the confusing multitude of potential donors, international organisations, universities and companies acting on very weak institutions in the S without knowing what is already going on (lack of a comprehensive inventory of all the activities).

"The South does not know what the results of the North are, nor does the South know what the mutual results are, nor does the North know what it's doing and what its priorities are." (Korte)

Secondly he criticised the unpredictability of funding and the weakness of national institutions in the S, leading to a weak formulation of their own national priorities and a dominating position of the donors who move into that vacuum.

Korte pleaded for fair conditions in the competition for research co-operation, transparency of supply and demand, and free choice of the actors to pick the best. This is seldom the case; often partners from the N crowd into countries with a favourable, stable political environment, good accessibility, communication systems, roads etc. There is often parallel support for highly fashionable international priority programmes (e.g. vaccine trials for malaria, HIV/AIDS or some parasitic diseases) and it even happens that money is paid to gain a stake in research opportunities. Sometimes the donor's activities become so dominant that local partners are distracted from their own research agenda. In order to get the research permit or the permit to publish results the names of the "partners" are just added to publications.

He stressed the need for long term support to research institutions in the S (15 to 20 years) allowing them to develop according to their own priorities and to learn to resist the influences stated previously. Korte ended by making two proposals:

- Donors and partners involved in specific research projects in DCs should contribute to a kind of capacity-building fund, in order not only to support a time-limited research programme, but also to strengthen the human resource base.
- A code of conduct should be formulated, laying down the principles of fair collaboration, including ethical considerations, in research partnerships between national and international partner institutions.

Charmes pointed towards structural adjustments in scientific research, particularly in Africa, due to severe financial restrictions which have led to the closing of a number of research institutions. Competition between institutes and researchers in the S for donors/partners from the N has become harder while at the same time many Northern countries question whether they still need and can afford specific research institutions dealing with development. This is true e.g. for ORSTOM, which used to work on the basis of subsidies from the government and now has to enter the market of bilateral and international donors in order to finance its research in the S. The pressure to obtain results usable for expert evaluations and decision-making has also greatly increased. Due to this fiercer competition within the N, the commercialisation of scientific research runs the risk of misusing partnerships as tickets for entering the research market. Similarly in the S, partnership can be misused to mobilise bilateral or multilateral funds for research on development. Such partnerships, where sellers & suppliers of partnerships on one hand and buyers & users on the other hand are simply buying and selling the right to collect data necessary to conduct the research programmes - without really involving the sellers in the process of capacity-building - should not be promoted at all.

"Research on development has to keep capacity building as an objective of primary importance, and not only to enhance the production of articles in scientific reviews." (Charmes)

In order to prevent brain drain and to support brain gain, France has created a specific agency giving financial and scientific support to research teams from the S on topics defined by themselves. This support is also oriented towards complementing the salaries of researchers in order to raise them to the level of the private sector or the domain of consulting.

Discussion

During discussion with the audience Said **Alloush**, from *Jordan* (Royal Scientific Society), came back to the waste of natural resources (cf. Chile) and suggested that the S should try to maximise the value-addition when exploiting national natural resources in order to "increase the backbone of the economy and to accumulate expertise and know-how". **Beye**, from *FAO/UNO*, pointed to the big differences in research capacity among the Southern countries and proposed building strong S-S co-operations (the Southern countries should show more initiative, relying on themselves and working together on terms of common interest). **Alhassan** from *Ghana* (CSIR) reacted to Howell's statement about the particularly weak position of his country and the problems related to partnership: 1) The positive effects of foreign help are mainly related to capacity-building (though the N benefits from training its own postgraduate students working on local problems, too). Some local graduate students have also started to benefit from the collaboration, particularly through "sandwich" training, where one part is done outside the country and the other part at home. 2) Although nationally relevant research issues and topics have been identified and prioritised, donors have not yet indicated which areas they will assist. 3) Training and education in particular fields, like engineering, manufacturing or management, are very weak; donors mainly support agricultural and environmental issues. 4) Interference in national programmes compromises their realisation; a solution could be to integrate donor assistance projects into national projects. 5) Friction between regional and CGIAR centres hinders the research, and is even sometimes intensified by anglophone-francophone competition, which causes uncertainty. **Carlman** from Sweden (SIDA) reacted to Bonte-Friedheims claim for "relevance first and quality second"; he preferred "a very relevant project of acceptable quality" to "an irrelevant project of high quality", but feared that "the day development-oriented research gets the reputation of being of second-rate research quality, it will be dead". Therefore relevant research of good quality should be promoted by attracting good researchers to important topics. **Howell** concluded the Panel by warning against exaggerating difficulties and too much self-criticism, advocating that what is working well should be emphasised.

compiled by Daniel Maselli

Swiss Policy in Partnership

Summary of the Forum Discussion

This discussion was in French. The main conclusions are presented in the overall Summary (Part I).

- Representatives of Swiss politics

Bernard Comby, *National Councillor, Member Swiss National Council*
Rudolf Nebiker, *National Councillor, Member Swiss National Council, President Governmental Consultative Commission for Development*
Thomas Onken, *Councillor of States, Member Swiss Council of States, President Commission for Science, Education and Culture of the Council of States*
Rosemarie Simmen, *Councillor of States, Member Swiss Council of States*

- Representatives of Swiss institutions concerned with research

André Aeschlimann, *President Research Council Swiss National Science Foundation*
Jean-François Giovannini, *Deputy Director Swiss Agency for Development and Co-operation*
Bruno Messerli, *Member Research Council Swiss National Science Foundation*
Francis Waldvogel, *President, Council of Federal Institutes of Technology*

- Moderator

Jean-Philippe Rapp, *Swiss Broadcasting Corporation*

Rapp ouvre le débat en citant Messerli dans son éditorial de *"Horizons"* (mars 1996) intitulé *"Responsable du monde de demain"* où il déplore la faible contribution de la Suisse à la coopération au développement à l'échelle européenne, ce qu'il avait particulièrement ressenti au Sommet de Rio en 1992: Que s'est-il passé depuis lors?

Messerli répond en faisant trois remarques:

❶ Les exportations suisses vers les pays en développement (PD) - sans compter les pays de l'OPEC - ont été de l'ordre de plus de 17% de l'exportation totale en 1995 causant un bilan en faveur de la Suisse de l'ordre de 10 milliards de CHF! Vu ce profit la Suisse

❷ Selon une déclaration récente d'un chef d'une des plus grandes banques suisses, il serait plus important de combattre le chômage et de relancer l'économie suisse que de s'occuper des problèmes environnementaux. Hors, pour Messerli, Rio a clairement démontré qu'on ne peut plus séparer ces domaines, car "un environnement détruit et des ressources épuisées coûteraient plus cher pour nous et plus encore pour les pays en développement". Il faut donc trouver de nouvelles stratégies "où l'économie, la politique et la science travaillent ensemble" pour résoudre ces problèmes à l'échelle globale.

❸ Chaque année des experts se disputent les chiffres de la future croissance économique suisse sans se poser la question s'il est encore judicieux de promouvoir une croissance étant donné l'état général de notre planète. Les pays industrialisés (PI) doivent s'interroger sur les conséquences d'une croissance économique, pour cela il importe d'informer en connaissance de cause tant le public que les politiciens et les représentants de l'économie suisse.

Finalement Messerli signale l'effort fourni par le Fonds National suisse (FNS) en partenariat avec la Direction du développement et de la coopération (DDC) à travers le Programme Prioritaire Environnement (PPE). Suite au Sommet de Rio le Module 7 "environnement et développement" lui a été ajouté comprenant actuellement environ 20 projets. Le budget (2-3 millions de CHF pour une durée de 3 ans) est partagé à part égale avec les partenaires du S.

Nebiker se préoccupe du déséquilibre budgétaire et remarque que les budgets dans le domaine de l'enseignement et de la recherche sont coupés dans presque tous les pays et que la Suisse n'y échappe pas! Mais cela permet de "repenser les choses essentielles" et de "se concentrer sur les priorités". Les ressources doivent être utilisées "d'une manière plus efficace en pensant aux générations futures". Bien que dans la loi fédérale sur la coopération, la promotion de l'échange scientifique figure parmi les priorités, il ne faut pas s'attendre à des miracles: "la Suisse est un petit pays"! Elle doit sa croissance et son rôle dans le monde "à ses relations dans le monde entier"; c'est pourquoi la Suisse ne peut pas se permettre de les limiter à l'Union Européenne, aux Etats Unis d'Amérique ou au Japon. Nebiker souligne l'importance et la responsabilité de l'échange scientifique et de la coopération tant avec les pays de l'Est qu'avec les partenaires d'Afrique, d'Asie ou d'Amérique latine.

Aeschlimann signale que les conséquences de coupures budgétaires exagérées se font ressentir à long terme. Il souligne que le Module 7 est financé à parts égales entre le FNS et la DDC. En plus de ce "partenariat helvético-suisse" les trois divisions classiques du FNS (sciences non-programmatiques) financent une série de projets de recherches fondamentales dans le Tiers Monde qui dépassent largement le montant du Module 7. Aeschlimann souhaiterait là aussi établir un partenariat avec la DDC et pense que le Conseil de la Recherche pourrait accorder une augmentation du budget de base "pour mieux réussir dans le Tiers Monde". Il soutient également une recherche fondamentale dans le Tiers Monde puisque "ce sont les pays du Sud eux-mêmes qui la réclament".

"Si dans quelques années l'économie de ce pays reprend et que nous n'avons pas les chercheurs qu'il faut, nous allons le payer très cher comparé aux économies que nous pensons faire aujourd'hui." (Aeschlimann)

"La recherche suisse doit forcément s'ouvrir - sur l'Europe comme sur le Tiers-Monde." (Aeschlimann)

Question **Rapp**: Dans les projets choisis par le FNS le facteur 'partenariat avec le Sud' joue-t-il un rôle important ou secondaire?

Aeschlimann répond que c'est "un facteur qu'il faut maintenant établir et faire connaître par les membres du Conseil de la recherche". Jusqu'à présent les fonds étaient surtout "destinés à soutenir la recherche suisse". Il est convaincu "qu'il faut changer de philosophie". **Messerli** ajoute que pour le Module 7 le partenariat est une condition "sine qua non".

Question **Rapp**: Le Parlement doit-il lui aussi changer sa philosopie?

Simmen réplique qu'il y a "une nette répartition des tâches entre les politiciens et les chercheurs et les milieux universitaires". Au Parlement revient de donner le cadre et aux milieux de la recherche de décider de la manière de procéder dans le partenariat avec leur partenaires au N comme au S. L'important c'est "qu'il y ait un effet durable et cohérent".

"La cohérence signifie que l'on se rende compte que le partenariat entre chercheurs vient au bout d'un long processus de développement." (Simmen)

Malgré le déséquilibre numérique entre chercheurs du N et du S (env. 30:1) Simmen signale qu'il ne faut pas oublier qu'avant de combler cette lacune il faut soutenir la scolarisation des enfants menacée faute de moyens financiers: "c'est là au fond que commence le partenariat dans la recherche". Il importe également d'obtenir une "cohérence entre formation et travail" permettant d'appliquer ce qui a été appris. Finalement les chercheurs ne doivent pas s'enfermer dans leur milieu scientifique mais garder les contacts noués avec le N.

Waldvogel affirme que le partenariat scientifique est devenu un thème important du débat des Ecoles Politechniques Fédérales (EPFs) en raison du processus de globalisation qui touche pratiquement tous les domaines, notamment au développement durable, à l'utilisation rationnelle des ressources et à la gestion correcte des déchets et du recyclage.

> *"Le partenariat pour moi n'est plus une vocation - il est devenu un acte rationnel, fondamental de la mise en réseau réciproque de tous nos différents systèmes."*
> (Waldvogel)

Il s'applique comme une discipline horizontale "qu'on ne peut pas simplement insérer dans un programme national ou dans un programme prioritaire mais qui devrait s'insérer dans les zones d'approche multidisciplinaire de toute la science". A première vue cela semble plus coûteux qu'une stratégie verticale, mais en fin de compte les résultats et les coûts donneront raison à cette approche.

> *"Je pense que le moment est venu que l'on considère le partenariat comme un engagement à part égale."*
> (Waldvogel)

Question **Rapp**: Les idées que vous venez de développer sont-elles des idées que l'on retrouve déjà profondément ancrées dans les EPFs ou commencent-elles seulement à être prises au sérieux?

Waldvogel répond que l'on est "en train de donner une impulsion dans cette direction" et qu'il s'agit là peut-être de "l'investissement principal que la Suisse peut faire" pour préparer la génération suivante à ce mode de penser.

Question **Rapp**: A quelle condition un partenariat vous paraît-il acceptable dans le cadre d'un projet d'une EPF?

Waldvogel, se rapportant aux conditions économiques et politiques, ne souhaiterait pas forcément plus de fonds de la part du Parlement, mais plutôt d'éviter la "stop and go policy" avec des reculs et des avances dans les budgets. Il préférerait disposer d'un montant garanti égal à la somme actuelle et serait prêt à fournir l'effort de partenariats internes avec l'économie et les secteurs privés.

Onken remarque que les buts d'une telle coopération scientifique entre le N et le S ne sont pas purement académiques mais qu'ils visent à une action politique et sociale. Il trouve que "la conscience dans les milieux politiques, n'est souvent pas à la hauteur quand il s'agit de ce point spécifique", c'est pourquoi "les chercheurs doivent faire plus de pression sur les politiciens" et les informer davantage. En vue d'une politique plus cohérente il est en faveur des budgets globaux permettant aux milieux de la recherche de décider eux-mêmes sur la distribution des fonds. Il sera alors intéressant de voir si les chercheurs donneront la priorité à des partenariats N-S.

"Je trouve que le partenariat est une chose absolument essentielle car beaucoup de problèmes que nous voudrions résoudre ensemble sont des problèmes liés aux disparités entre le N et le S dont les solutions peuvent être trouvées uniquement ensemble." (Onken)

Onken transmet également - au nom de **Haering-Binder** - le désir que de plus grands efforts soient entrepris pour intégrer les femmes dans les projets de recherche.

La première remarque de **Comby** se base sur un rapport à l'intention du "Club of Rome" intitulé "*La révolution aux pieds nus*" (SCHNEIDER) qui prétend que suite au choc pétrolier de 1974 le dialogue N-S est devenu une *confrontation N-S*. La politique d'aide au développement aurait été plutôt un échec qu'un succès favorisant souvent les grands projets au détriment des petits, avec toutes les conséquences écologiques, sociales et autres. Ainsi un responsable camerounais aurait dit: "on ne peut pas lutter contre les grands économistes internationaux qui ne connaissent pas les problèmes des paysans ... alors nous avons pensé que c'était aux paysans de faire des projets de développement, d'essayer de les faire aboutir, de s'entre-aider plutôt que d'attendre que l'aide vienne d'un grand projet". Comby favorise le concept "d'auto-développement"; il lui paraît à mieux de pourvoir aux besoins des populations locales.

Vu les dépenses actuelles de l'Aide aux réfugiés (CHF 900 millions/an) et de l'Aide au développement (CHF 1'200 millions/an) **Comby** suggère de plafonner le premier montant et d'essayer d'augmenter le second tout en étant le plus efficace possible. Il propose d'évaluer systématiquement (en commun avec des chercheurs du S) tous les projets de développement à l'aide d'un pourcent du budget.

Sur cela **Giovannini** déclare que "les motifs pour lesquelles le Gouvernement suisse donne des moyens pour la Coopération au développement ne sont pas essentiellement de nature éthique mais plutôt des motifs de communauté de destin". Le mandat légal de la DDC est de favoriser le développement par les propres forces des PD et non pas de résoudre des problèmes. La loi de 1976 demande d'aider les pays à développer leurs propres forces et capacités dans tous les domaines. Ceci explique l'importance accordée à la recherche de la part de la DDC ainsi que son intérêt vis-à-vis de la stratégie et son intention d'établir une étroite collaboration avec la communauté scientifique suisse. Giovannini est persuadé qu'une partie importante de la recherche en Suisse a pour thème des questions d'ordre général qui touchent aux PD et qu'il y a là un potentiel de coopération considérable.

"La DDC est partie prenante dans une coopération entre institutions de recherche du S et du N - elle est prête à financer la partie du Sud." (Giovannini)

La DDC est intéressée à établir des collaborations semblables à celle du Module 7 dans d'autres domaines à condition que: 1) le type de recherche réponde aux priorités des pays partenaires, 2) une masse critique puisse être atteinte de manière à ce que les résultats obtenus soient significatifs et utiles aux partenaires, 3) l'organisation soit efficace et que l'institution sache au mieux utiliser les capacités existantes au N comme au S et s'insérer dans les réseaux internationaux de recherche.

Rapp signale la publication d'un article dans le Journal de Genève (6 mars 1996) intitulé "isolée en Europe, la recherche suisse collabore avec le Sud - une occasion pour la Suisse de rattraper le retard pris sur le reste de l'Europe". Question Rapp: La Suisse actuellement fait-elle suffisament d'efforts dans le domaine du développement?

Messerli compare tout d'abord les efforts de la Suisse à ceux de la Suède et des Pays Bas présentés lors de la première journée de la Conférence. Il constate que la Suisse est malgré tout "restée un peu derrière les autres" et que dans divers domaines elle a beaucoup à apprendre du S.

Pour **Waldvogel** les problèmes tels que la surpopulation et la pauvreté (cf. Uma Lele) touchent particulièrment le S et font du partenariat une condition sine qua non de la survie de tous. C'est pourquoi la Suisse a un intérêt à soutenir les efforts au S et à augmenter sa contribution. Il ne faut pas forcément des fonds supplémentaires, mais plutôt un changement de paradigme. Cela signifie une sensibilisation de tout le monde vis-à-vis des problèmes globaux futurs

Comby signale que la Suisse a adhéré en décembre 1995 à l'Agence de coopération culturelle et technique de la francophonie devenant l'un des principaux contributeurs (environ 80% des fonds vont aux pays du S pour soutenir des projets de développement).

Aeschlimann signale que le FNS est actuellement en train de discuter de ce partenariat et de l'ouverture vis-à-vis du Tiers Monde. Personnellement il est convaincu que le FNS ne fait pas assez. Mais puisqu'on ne peut pas demander au Parlement d'augmenter sans cesse les budgets "il faut faire autrement avec ce qu'on a". C'est pourquoi il propose de revoir la distribution de certains crédits en faveur de programmes de recherche dans le Tiers Monde.

"La recherche fondamentale précède toujours la recherche pratique." (Aeschlimann)

Simmen - est d'avis que le titre de l'article ne signifie pas que le partenariat scientifique avec le S puisse être le moyen d'échapper au blocage européen. Il traduit plutôt le souci de résoudre des problèmes là où c'est le plus urgent. La question n'est donc pas si la recherche et les projets sont européens ou non, mais s'ils sont nécessaires d'un point de vue scientifique et pratique.

Giovannini pense qu'il y a effectivement un grand potentiel de collaboration qu'il faut saisir - le Module 7 et les nombreuses requêtes intéressantes présentées l'ont démontré. Pour y répondre la DDC est "prête à déplacer les ressources".

Onken réagit à l'intervention d'Aeschlimann en disant que le Parlement discute le budget mais qu'il ne touche pas à l'autonomie du FNS qui garde une grande marge de manoeuvre. Il pense "qu'il serait possible de faire plus", que "l'on devrait faire plus" et que "le FNS devrait donner une plus grande priorité à ce domaine".

"Le Parlement ne dicte pas les priorités mis à part peut-être les Programmes Prioritaires." (Onken)

Messerli pense qu'il y a des barrières au N comme au S: "Notre mentalité n'est pas encore orientée vers des projets en partenariat" et "la recherche dans le Tiers Monde est souvent considérée comme une recherche de deuxième ou troisième qualité qu'on ne peut pas financer". C'est pourquoi "la pression de la politique envers la science" n'est pas mauvaise. Au Sud c'est le contraire: "La science n'a pas le prestige nécessaire - elle est isolée et n'a pas d'argent". Il manque la pression des scientifiques envers la politique.

Dans le cadre de la **discussion** avec l'auditoire **Musy** (EPFL) considère la recherche fondamentale comme étant certe importante "mais les pays du S ont surtout besoin d'une recherche appliquée avec un transfert rapide". Il pose deux questions: A l'adresse d'*Aeschlimann*: *"Puisque la DDC se déclare prête à financer les partenaires du S pour des projets de recherche appliquée, qui va prendre en charge les coûts des chercheurs suisses étant donné que le FNS accprde un soutien prioritaire à la recherche fondamentale mais pas à la recherche appliquée?"* A l'adresse de *Waldvogel: "Comment peut-on valoriser les chercheurs qui sont impliqués dans ces recherches appliquées du moment où ils n'ont pas la possibilité de publier des articles scientifiques de très haut niveau puisque le caractère même de la recherche ne le leur permet pas de le faire?"*
Aeschlimann réplique que jusqu'à présent la majorité des projets (p.e. au Centre d'Ifakara en Tanzanie et au Centre Suisse de Recherche Scientifique en Côte d'Ivoire) avaient toujours une phase appliquée et que "ce n'est que maintenant que je constate à quel point nous avons aussi besoin d'une recherche fondamentale dans les pays du S - ne serait-ce que pour la formation". **Waldvogel** est de l'avis qu'il "revient aux autorités supérieures des structures de recherche" d'essayer de soutenir des projets plus appliqués et donc "d'honorer le caractère créatif de ce type de recherche et de réalisation". Il cite comme exemple la pollution du Tiers Monde par des mines anti-personnelles où l'EPFL avec l'aide de fondations externes et privées a réussi à financer un projet de recherche.
Comby partage l'avis de Musy et privilégierait davantage la recherche appliquée dans les pays du S pour combler le retard économique vis-à-vis du N.
Alloush (RSJ, Jordan) thinks that "it is very important that projects - either applied or basic - have an impact on society in the South, in order to create credibility for scientific research and for its institutions".
Cetto (UNAM, Mexico) proposed the creation of a programme allowing young staff from the N to "spend one or two years in a developing country, when they can already teach something but they also have still a lot to learn" since "very often, a good research partnership starts with a personal contact and with individual experience".
Auroi (IUED, membre CO Conférence) plaide en faveur d'une plus grande transparence: d'une part il faut que la Suisse fasse savoir davantage à l'étranger ce qu'elle fait comme recherche dans le domaine du développement et d'autre part la Suisse doit mieux se

rendre compte de ce qui se fait dans d'autres pays à cet égard. Il plaide en faveur d'une continuation de cette conférence sous une forme à déterminer.

Rapp reprend une question du public liée au fait que "les fonds de la recherche dépendent en bonne partie des politiciens": Les membres du lobby 'recherche en faveur ou en collaboration avec le Tiers Monde' au sein du Parlement est-il plutôt en voie d'extension ou plutôt d'extinction?

Comby indique "qu'il est très difficile de mener une discussion comme celle d'aujourd'hui"; cependant "une espèce de lobby défendant la recherche et la formation en Suisse" s'est formée qui obtient des résultats positifs depuis quelques années. Mais il importe que les responsables du domaine scientifique interviennent eux-mêmes régulièrement pour se battre afin d'obtenir davantage de moyens financiers et qu'ils devraient procéder à une auto-critique.

Hountondji (Bénin) signale "qu'il est extrêmement dangereux de consacrer et de perpétuer l'actuelle division internationale du travail scientifique qui consiste à réserver, aux pays du N le monopole d'inventions scientifiques et à confiner les pays du S par l'application des résultats de cette invention. Même lorsque l'on doit simplement appliquer, il faut au moins savoir ce que l'on applique!" Il perçoit comme véritables problèmes entre autre la difficulté d'accumuler et de capitaliser le savoir au S.

D'après **Agustoni-Phang** (Zürich) le véritable problème du renforcement des capacités de recherche n'est pas celui du manque d'une masse critique mais plutôt le fait que "la masse est parfois plus intelligente que l'État" et que "la démocratie manque!" Tandis que "dans les pays du Sud l'Etat dit au peuple *ferme ta gueule* ici dans les pays démocratiques du Nord il lui dit *cause toujours*."

compiled by Daniel Maselli

The Working Groups

According to the concept of the Conference, the Working Groups constituted the core of the event. The conveners intended to make a sharp contrast with the first part, where selected experts had the opportunity to express their views and to share experience acquired in both North and South. After the introductory statements, a panel discussion, a round table talk and the forum addressing Swiss policy, the working groups offered a platform for exchange and discussion to all participants. In this setting, the conveners aimed at reaching goals 2 and 3 of the Conference: to hear from researchers about the experience they have gained hitherto with research partnership, and to jointly define ways in which research collaboration among dissimilar partners can be carried out, for example with new forms of institutional partnership, capacity-building and support of institutions, as well as adequate follow-up mechanisms.

Initially, 8 working groups were foreseen. However, the number finally grew to 10. In order to meet a request from participants from West Africa, representatives of the Swiss Federal Polytechnic at Lausanne launched an initiative to offer a French-speaking working group, and as a large number of participants registered for working group A (research agendas), it was decided that a second group should address this topic.

In order to prepare the field adequately for discussions, to provide some signposts, and to prevent the discussion becoming diffuse, the Working Groups were organised according to the following pattern. An *Initiator* had the challenging task of outlining briefly the issues linked to the topic to be discussed; after this introduction, two *Co-Moderators* (one from the North and one from the South) directed the discussions. These two experts were also responsible for the elaboration of the report to be presented to the audience at the next day's plenary session. Moreover, it was expected that this team would submit a report to the conveners. Besides the issues raised, this paper should show explicitly the points of convergence, and the differences that came to light, as well as the suggestions or recommendations forwarded.

This section of the proceedings is based on the material handed over to the conveners. However, due to considerable differences in form, content, and style, the reports submitted have been reviewed critically, and the most important elements have been synthesised and rearranged. Each chapter starts with a the outline given to the participants (box), and the names of the persons in charge of the Working Group. These presentations do not really focus on the interactions which occurred between different parties but shed light on the issues raised, the procedure followed and the divergent views (if available), the results of the discussions which took place, and the suggestions forwarded by the participants.

A Research Agendas

Who defines, who promotes, and who funds research agendas in the South, how is information disseminated, and what are the expected results and benefits? Priorities of research as seen from the South.

> There is an undeniable uniformity in the topics that international research programmes focus on at any one time. Either one group of issues or a set of related themes dominates. Thus, in recent years some new issues - especially in the domains of macro-economic policy, good governance and participation, as well as global environmental change - became subjects of public concern whereas some others fell out of fashion. In some cases, it can be observed that the themes promoted are closely linked to the agendas of major international conferences. Their emergence and disappearance reflects the life cycles of such events.
>
> One of the points of interest is to gain some insight into the process of emergence and diffusion of these internationally-recognised agendas. It is questionable whether these emerging trends reflect real needs and lead to a strengthening of research capacities. Moreover, rapidly changing priorities and paradigms create a merry-go-round whereby new themes and approaches are introduced before research on previous key issues has been accomplished, and before sound solutions can be designed and successfully implemented. In this workshop, a critical discussion will therefore address the question of how and by whom these specific themes are defined, and how they are promoted. Participants should evaluate the expected results and benefits and compare them to priorities of research as seen from the South and from the North.

Initiator: **Yusuf Bangura**, *United Nations Research Institute for Social Development UNRISD, Geneva*

Co-Moderators A1: **Frederick Bugenyi**, *Fisheries Research Institute, Jinja (Uganda)*
Richard Gerster, *Swiss Coalition of Development Organisations, Bern*

Co-Moderators A2: **Urs Geiser**, *Geography Dept., University of Zurich*
Martin Khor, *Penang Consumer's Association*

Procedure in the group discussion

Yusuf Bangura's input covered a wide range of topics, not only the definition of research agendas. The 25 participants of this working group - of whom 8 were representatives from the South - reviewed the aspects he had addressed. In many cases, experiences of the participants confirmed Dr. Bangura's statements.

Issues discussed

- *Definition of research agendas*
    - clear-cut research policies either do not exist in the South or are ignored by organisations and researchers of the North; donors define programmes in most cases
    - agendas are rarely demand-driven
    - large political organisations such as the World Bank and the WTO operate as trend-setters
    - agendas are defined by many actors with unequal power and influence but also with unequal capacities
    - growing dominance of geopolitical forces and global themes limits the scope for influence by researchers themselves; they are forced to join the bandwagon
- *Consequences for research implementation*
    - often researchers from the South are seen as technicians or junior associates but not as equal partners
    - Northern researchers appear to be powerful because they deal with theoretical and conceptual issues; Southern partners collect data and implement actions
    - the prevailing complexity and heterogeneity lead to functional misunderstandings
    - due to precarious salaries, Southern researchers "have no time" to care about agendas and institutions: they are drawn either to administrative work or the writing of consultancy reports
    - the prevailing labour division does not enhance capacity-building in the South
    - capacity-building is not necessarily a "side-effect" in a learning-by-doing setting; it needs funds and action plans
- *Funding*
    - funding has to be long term
    - only considerable autonomy in funding leads to the South developing its own research agendas

Conclusions and recommendations
- partners from the South have to be represented on management boards of international donor agencies
- in particular, young researchers have to be encouraged and introduced into current agendas
- the private sector in the South should get more involved in the setting of agendas, however, the expected material and symbolic benefits have to be spelled out
- all parties involved have to agree on the goals and the evaluative criteria for planned or ongoing partnerships
- agendas have to emerge from the South and must be negotiated in an open dialogue: clear objectives, national priorities or field realities are decisive for appropriate and acceptable agenda-setting

B Pitfalls of Partnership

Covered leadership, residual paternalism, data for donations.

> During the last few decades, large amounts of money have been spent on funding all kinds of research and collaborative efforts. However, in many fields, the results are rather disillusioning. In developing countries the state of teaching and research institutions has been deteriorating continuously, and the brain drain has increased. Researchers from the South often blame their colleagues and donor agencies from the North for pursuing their own interests. They feel that they are being instrumentalised and exploited for the sake of bypassing regulations and cultural obstacles. Moreover, a "data-for-donations" attitude is widespread. This does not allow for capacity- and institution-building, and reflects the fact that needy institutions in the South are in a very exposed position.
> However, according to the ideals of collaboration, research partnership is a reciprocal process. Therefore, research subjects have to be identified jointly, and the design of the research process must acknowledge the potentials of both partners, and aim at an equal distribution of the benefits.
> Participants in this workshop will review current problems in research collaboration such as residual paternalism, unilateral utility, "data-for-donations" settings, the "tarmac or white collar bias" or the "academy bias", etc. They may also evaluate whether teaching and training programmes or other forms of transfer are appropriate to overcome the widespread pitfalls.

Initiator: **Ruth Egger**, Intercoopération, Bern
Co-Moderators: **Oumar Niangado**, Institut d'économie rurale, Bamako (Mali)
Stephen C. Stearns, University of Basle

Procedure in the group discussion

Ruth Egger gave a presentation that met with broad agreement. In it, she presented a model of how the concept of research partnership can be implemented. The discussion that followed mainly addressed six issues: the role of cultural differences, reciprocity in relationships, the disruptive effects of major investments, criteria for good partnership, patents and property rights, and, finally, research and/or investments. However, instead of enumerating pitfalls, participants tended to highlight normative concepts and proposals of how to overcome the prevailing pitfalls.

Issues discussed

- *The role of cultural differences*
  - stakeholders have different concepts of research; predominance and overestimation of Northern methodologies and values and underestimation of indigenous local, traditional knowledge is still common
  - arrogance and paternalism are widespread in the North
  - research policies are different; an equal dialogue has to be established in order to find an initial definition, shared by all parties involved
- *Reciprocity in relationships*
  - the agenda and the contract must be negotiable and negotiated: a clear understanding has to be achieved by both partners
  - money flows have to be transparent, and the management accountable
  - exchange of scholars facilitates the reaching of international standards and prevents brain drain
- *Disruptive effects of major investments*
  - far-reaching negative effects of major investments (e.g. structural adjustment programmes) must be more fully appreciated
  - researchers jump on new bandwagons either due to precariousness of salaries, desire to generate income, or opportunism, and abandon research teams or neglect duties and cause indirect/hidden costs
- *Criteria for good partnership*
  - joint selection of topic - demand orientation
  - no hidden agenda or vested interests but clarification of expectations and ownership
  - not according to fashions, but to strategic interests of beneficiaries

- complementarity/subsidiarity to existing personnel and networks
- long term commitment and equal benefits on both sides
- evaluation of progress and impact on recipient culture
- gender issue considered
- make the invisible visible

Points of disagreement
- the issue of patents and property rights: some felt that it was not an issue; other felt that no money should be spent on research projects that would produce patented results that would not be published and shared
- location of and distinction between basic and applied research
- good partnership requires a good environment for investment

Recommendations
- end-users should be involved by donors and by their own countries in research policy formulation
- 1% of research budgets should be set aside for capacity-building in the South
- Switzerland must define its research policy with the South and make this policy known so that projects will be implemented accor-ding to these principles

C Constraints on Research Partnership
Institutional, structural, financial and discipline-related aspects

> Research partnership is often hampered by the incompatible institutional profiles and different structural settings of the partners. Whereas research is often initiated by universities or broadly-based project teams in the North, in the South they have to collaborate with government-related organisations which operate on the basis of sectoral policies. Another problematic issue is the disproportional input of financial support. This leads, in many cases, to a situation where researchers from the North define the subjects and methods of a study, and also control the dissemination of results. With respect to funding, a certain protectionism is undeniable in industrialised countries; it is often asserted that money spent for collaboration with partners in the South is wasted because it does not directly serve the interests of the country which raises the funds. In addition, some disciplines are perceived as being less useful than others. They therefore have problems with funding and, consequently, may not be able to build up capacities in the South. This applies especially to the humanities.

> In this workshop, the participants will discuss current constraints and elaborate ways to overcome them. Participants may also assess the question of whether research collaboration should be carried out on the basis of bilateral agreements, or whether it can only be effective when embedded in large international or multilateral programmes.

Initiator: **K.N. Nair**, Centre for Development Studies, Thiruvananthapuram, India

Co-Moderators: **George K. King'oriah**, Egerton University, Kenya
Peter Trutmann, Centre for International Agriculture, Zurich

Issues discussed (and agreed on)

- *Institutional constraints*
  - differences in North and South (private - public)
  - large number of constraints, constraints increasing
  - restructuring needed, especially in the South

- *Financial constraints*
  - economic reforms and reduction of funds in the North
  - greater market orientation - higher transaction costs
  - demand driven research has negative effects on those who cannot pay

- *Asymmetry of information*
  - Southern scientists often lack access to information
  - case of journals discussed
  - networking, improvement of quality of journals in the South and improved access to lists

- *Incentive structure*
  - inadequate incentives exist to encourage good research and partnerships
  - conditional funding in which incentives are embedded, is needed

- *Hierarchical structures*
  - especially characteristic of institutes in South
  - cause high transaction costs
  - need to revitalise non-governmental research organisations (e.g. foundations might provide more clearing houses)

- *Political constraints*
  - unstable governments - unfavourable climate for research and funding

- **Scientific priority setting regarding national policies**
  - often research is not included in national priorities of the South
  - more lobbying needed for research in general
- **Research management**
  - increased responsibilities require research management
  - research manager positions are rarely found but there is a need
- **Forms of cooperation**
  - merits of bilateral and multilateral research
  - variability in problems requires flexible approaches

Conclusions and recommendations

- need for institutional restructuring of research activities
- need to lobby politicians at national level to include research in the national priorities
- need for reward systems that encourage partnership and good science (e.g. conditional funding)
- need for awareness that the move to competitive, demand driven funding (private industry) carries transaction costs which will discriminate against those who cannot pay
- need to increase the transparency of funding
- need to encourage networking to improve South-South and South-North cooperation and information exchange
- need to remain flexible in terms of cooperation (e.g. bilateral or multilateral)

D South-South Research Collaboration

Potential and problems

> Despite numerous attempts and agreements, South-South research collaboration has never really developed its potential. A range of problems arise from language barriers and communication difficulties between countries and continents. However, the effectiveness of South-South collaboration is also hampered by different states of development of potential partners, disparities in the resources they can mobilise, and also conflicting interests. In this respect, stakes and commitments may sharply differ when there is competition for comparative advantages and research funds.

> However, South-South research collaboration is important because developing countries clearly have some scientific goals, interests and needs that are different from those proposed and financed by industrialised countries, donor agencies and multilateral agencies from the North. There is a radically self-reliant position that postulates that the North should be kept out of research in the South. In order to reconcile the positions, the initiative recently launched by COMSAT (Commission on Science and Technology for Sustainable Development in the South) to create a network for the promotion of indigenous capacity-building is an appropriate and commendable step in the right direction.
>
> The aim of this workshop is to enumerate the major obstacles to South-South collaboration, and to formulate sound propositions to enhance such collaboration. Moreover, this workshop should offer a forum for a constructive discussion of the strategies and means that the North could apply in order to encourage and develop collaborative efforts among partners in the South.

Initiator: **Jorge Eduardo Allende**, University of Chile
Co-Moderators: **Khotso Mokhele**, Foundation for Research Development, South Africa
Jacques Forster, IUED, Geneva

Issues discussed

- *Reasons for South-South collaboration*
    - cooperation is vital to define priorities for topics of research
    - neighbouring countries often have common cultures
    - countries often face common problems
    - South-South collaboration can help to reach the critical mass of resources needed to tackle interdisciplinary problems and ambitious projects; thus it can help to achieve sustainability by strengthening the scientific community
    - no disadvantages for the participating countries are identified
    - Southern scientists working in the North could play a key role
- *Key limiting factors to South-South collaboration*
    - lack of information or knowledge of neighbouring countries
    - lack of awareness of common problems
    - great difficulties in communication due to poor infrastructure
    - political problems within and between countries
    - absence of official policies, institutions, programmes, funding
    - lack of financial support from regional and external sources
    - poor capacities and adverse attitude of scientific community
    - lack of organisation of the scientific community

Recommendations
- elaborate directories of research institutions, evaluated lists of scientists and research profiles
- develop regional environmental councils composed of scientists as well as networks of NGOs, foundations
- develop regional pools of expertise
- e-mail seems to be the best solution to overcome the lack of communication infrastructure in terms of cost and access
- facilitate access to modern information technologies; bring them within reach of poor countries and their scientific communities
- emphasise the necessity of encouraging the free circulation of scientists and scientific information
- design mechanisms and policies by which this can be implemented
- create groups to implement these recommendations
- scientific community has to insist that scientific activities know no borders
- scientific community needs to be organised to defend these recommendations
- funding from the South is necessary
- a certain percentage of funds from bilateral and multilateral agencies should be earmarked for South-South cooperation
- greater co-ordination of research funding
- triangular cooperation combining North-South and South-South cooperation should be encouraged
- institutions independent from governments should be promoted

E   Aims of Capacity and Institution Building
Expectations and strategies

> It can hardly be contested that research institutes and organisations in developing countries often suffer from problems such as empty cash boxes, brain drain, poor expertise, and weak structures. In order to compensate for these comparative disadvantages, many collaborative research projects dedicate part of their efforts to capacity-building and institutional development. However, the goals of this support are rarely considered. It is likely that donors will implement programmes according to their respective policies.

> Furthermore their efforts often reflect the fact that some money has to be invested in this domain in order to obtain research clearances. In such a setting, donors lack policies which take into account the long term perspectives of the institution concerned and its potential contribution to solving societal and environmental problems. There is a tendency to ignore the fact that universities in the South may have orientations other than those of industrialised countries.
>
> In this workshop, participants will a) discuss the capacity- and institution-building issue by asking critical questions about the scope of the assistance given, how enduring the results are, and the legitimisation, aims and hidden agendas of the donors, b) outline prerequisites for sound research and training curricula, and c) address the question of whether current schemes of collaboration actually prevent the South from developing centres of excellence.

Initiator: **Roland Waast**, *ORSTOM, Paris*
Co-Moderators: **Dyna Carol Arhin**, *LSHTM, Ghana/London*
Roland Schertenleib, *EAWAG, Dübendorf/Zurich*

Issues discussed

After discussing the meaning of capacity- and institution-building with regard to research partnerships, special emphasis was given to the following points:

- *National policies*
    - need for national strategies/plans/policies developed in consultation with all the actors involved, including the research community and the potential users of the research results
- *Existing capacities*
    - their identification
    - their enhancement leading to a critical mass

Recommendations

- *Addressed to all actors*
    - partnerships should be based on
    - research should be designed to achieve measurable outputs with regard to capacity-building
- *Addressed to the donor community*
    - more funds should be available for Southern researchers to prepare research protocols

- more funds should be managed by partners in the South
- Southern researchers currently working in the North should be enabled to return home and be focal points for continuing partnerships
- some funds should be available without the condition that the Southern institution must collaborate with Northern institution(s) from a specific country

- **Addressed to the partner in the North**
  - not only junior but also senior researchers from the institution in the North should spend adequate time in the South
- **Addressed to the partner in the South**
  - researchers should take the responsibility for marketing their research to national policy makers and potential funders

F   Equity in Reward Systems
Ownership and value of data and results

This workshop will address the issue of ownership and value of data and results. In critical comments the current situation is often compared to a colonial setting: knowledge is extracted in the South in the same way as minerals, and it is then processed and sold in the North. Since the important markets for scientific expertise are in industrialised countries, very little will find its way back. Whereas regulations for the handling of material property exist, intellectual property and traditional knowledge are not adequately protected. This applies to knowledge production in developing countries in general, as well as to the findings and writings of individual researchers in particular. Moreover, in the South there is often little respect for research because it is neither a profitable activity nor immediately useful. In some cases, governments may not be able to perceive the potential uses and benefits of results, or have no means to enforce equitable rewarding. Researchers suffer not only from a discouraging environment, but also because of their remoteness, which frequently prevents them from access to international discussion fora and publications.

> This issue is complex and sensitive. It is linked to political conditions, and also reflects academic competitiveness and reveals the consequences of poor standards, dependency, and other obstacles. Centres of excellence in the North define the mainstream(s), and the periphery has no adequate means to keep pace. The participants should approach these questions and evaluate platforms of exchange which provide both equitable benefits and sustainable development.

Initiator: *Paulin A. Hountondji*, University of Benin
Co-Moderators: *Guéladio Cissé*, EIER, Ouagadougou (Burkina Faso)
Jean-Bernard Dubois, Swiss Agency for Development and Cooperation SDC, Berne

Issues discussed

- *Scientific "division of labour"*
  - some kinds of scientific labour seem to restrict the monopoly of invention to the North
  - the South is expected to supply data and occasionally apply the results of research
  - research in the South, like education systems, remains basically extroverted, servicing the North instead of capacity-building
  - Southern research is generally committed to asking questions and solving problems that are of interest to the North, and bound to use instruments designed and made in the North
  - the inclusion by a Northern counterpart of partners in the South may be used just to make a project acceptable to funding institutions

- *Economic imbalances*
  - lack of economic incentives for research in the South
  - great imbalance in salaries in partnership projects
  - difficult general living and working conditions of local researchers in the South

- *Intellectual property*
  - intellectual property rights and patents procedures are not entirely familiar to researchers in the South
  - "traditional" knowledge among communities in the South is continually appropriated by "modern" researchers, and little benefit from that finds its way back

- **Remoteness**
  - remoteness of researchers in the South prevents them from access to international discussion fora and publications

Recommendations
- the definition by developing countries themselves of consistent research and science policies is a prerequisite of scientific development in the South
- mutual respect for each partner's capabilities
- research programmes should include scholarships for local staff
- donor institutions should ensure effective follow-up support of former students
- additional resources are required to develop autonomous research capacities
- donors and scientists must recognise traditional knowledge, respect it as the property of individuals or communities, and make sure that the owner(s) of this knowledge benefit from research
- scientists must acknowledge the sources of their knowledge, e.g. traditional healers
- salary structures need careful consideration
- results should be accessible to the South and especially to the public concerned
- scientists need to be informed about possibilities of protecting intellectual property
- scientific software in the South must be strengthened: networks, journals, conferences

G Transfer of Findings

Effects on local populations, centres of excellence and national policies

> Unilateral funding may lead to an uneven distribution of the findings and the benefits of research carried out in the South. For researchers, reaching an international audience is often the first priority. They frequently lack appropriate strategies for dissemination in the country where the study was made, or simply neglect this aspect. Moreover, it has been observed that there is a widening gap between researchers, their agendas and the needs of the respective countries and local populations. Since trickle-down effects reaching actors at local level constitute the exception rather than the rule, these circumstances do not allow for sustainable development.

> Therefore, participants in this session will draw up a list of current obstacles which hamper the transfers needed at the various levels. With the aim of improving the transfer process, they may discuss their own experiences and assess the viability and practicability of alternative models, e.g. the creation of regional or problem-oriented centres of excellence, local and regional networks in collaboration with NGOs, national transfer organisations, and international networks and their integration into national policies. They may further reflect upon the role of experts: should they retreat and no longer do co-ordination jobs, or keep a bridging activity which brings them into direct contact with crucial issues and perceptions, and the strategies of those who are concerned?

Initiator: **Lotfia el Nadi**, *Cairo University and University of Qatar*
Co-Moderators: **Francis Ndegwa Gichuki**, *University of Nairobi*
Marcel Tanner, *Swiss Tropical Institute, Basle*

Issues discussed and agreed on

- **Uneven distribution of findings and benefits**
    - research is mostly undertaken by scientists from the North and disseminated in journals with limited circulation in the South
    - research is mostly not problem-oriented and does not address specific needs of the targeted beneficiaries
    - there are financial, social, institutional and logistic constraints to technology transfer
    - the human and institutional capacities needed for the transfer of findings are inadequate
- **Prerequisites of transfer/exchange**
    - trust
    - mind-matching
    - commitment of all involved
    - good communication (e-mail, journals, meetings)
    - resources available (human, funds, time frames)
    - consensus on research topics, aims and implications

Unresolved issues/disagreements

- responsibility (who, at what level, to what extent)?
- who are the "ambassadors" of findings - necessarily researchers, or good managers and promoters?

Recommendations
- adopt a view of exchange on the basis of the prerequisites stated
- address all levels of transfer: research institutions, decision makers, involved communities
- consider all players (mainly beneficiaries at all levels)
- formal or informal research collaborators in the South should participate in problem definition, synthesis of findings and their application to local problems
- research should be demand-driven and the beneficiaries participate in problem definition, priority setting and feed-back processes
- develop national research priorities
- accountability and transparency should be promoted
- strategies for alleviating socio-cultural constraints affecting the dissemination of findings should be incorporated in research plans
- local methods and financial resources should be mobilised to facilitate dissemination
- ensure regular consultation between researchers, agencies and beneficiaries in order to identify institutional and policy constraints, and strategies for alleviating cultural constraints
- encourage publication in local and regional journals by strengthening their editorial capacities and expanding circulation

H   Access to Knowledge and Results
Tackling the remoteness of researchers in the South

> One of the major obstacles to sustainable development of the research institutions in the South is their relative remoteness in comparison to the centres of excellence in the North. As a consequence of this distance and lack of financial resources, individual researchers as well as institutions suffer from poor equipment as well as out-dated literature and material, i.e. attending congresses is not affordable, fax communication is too expensive, journals are not available, and electronic mailing networks unknown or not accessible. Researchers in the South therefore face almost insurmountable obstacles in their work, for they have no appropriate means to follow the advance of science and learn about newly emerging trends. Since they are not exposed to international standards, the trickle-down effects which would improve the current situation in teaching, training and policy design, and enhance capacity-building, cannot take place.

> It is not contested that the creation and promotion of networks and electronic conferences may, in some cases, be implemented successfully. However, significant financial and technical inputs are necessary. Participants are requested to delineate sound and sustainable solutions which would provide access to the current state of knowledge, recent scientific findings and data.

Initiator:	**Bui thi Lang**, *Committee for Science and Technology, Ho Chi Minh City (Vietnam)*
Co-Moderators:	**Emanuel Ndione**, *ENDA, Dakar (Senegal)*
	Carol Priestley, *International African Institute, London*
	Rudolf Baumgartner, *NADEL/ETH, Zurich*

Issues discussed

- **Mediation between various knowledge systems**
  - integration of indigenous into national and regional knowledge and vice versa
- **Responsibility for research and information**
  - (joint) responsibility of politicians, decision makers and scientists
- **Need for an information infrastructure**
  - publication
  - access to information
  - utilisation and dissemination of information
- **Role of supporting partners**
  - lack of national research policies, difficulty of choice of partners

Recommendations

- be aware of the cultural dimensions of local knowledge systems and the role they play in the allocation of status and power
- find ways to evaluate information, especially when introducing it into local knowledge systems
- information needs of collaborators in the South should be recognised as legitimate
- there should be an on-going evaluation of information needs
- gaps in research should be identified and addressed jointly
- results of scientific research of the South should not necessarily be validated using criteria of the North
- scientists, researchers and supporting partners must promote the generation of information in national or regional knowledge systems

- national and regional scientific journals have an important role to play, both in dissemination of research results and in promoting further research
- research partners from the North should also be encouraged to publish in national and regional publications
- priority should be given to the training of information gatekeepers
- research partners must keep each other informed of relevant information
- the relevance of information has to be evaluated with regard to local needs
- developing countries might need to identify national or regional focal points for distribution of information, taking language into account
- new technologies offer alternative sources of information but do not provide all the solutions (Internet is not able to validate local knowledge systems)
- donors should be encouraged to support the development of indigenous publication
- supporting partners can also assist with the careful introduction of appropriate information technology

I Le rôle de l'intermédiation de la recherche pour le développement
French speaking working group - Atelier en langue française

Comment et qui peut assurer l'intermédiation entre les partenaires chercheurs universitaires et les autres acteurs du développement, en particulier les populations et leurs autorités locales et régionales? Si l'on admet que l'un des objectifs principaux des partenariats de recherche est l'amélioration des conditions de vie des populations, on constate que de nombreux projets n'ont pas ou partiellement atteint cet objectif. Dans de nombreux cas, on se rend compte que le passage de la recherche à son application est difficile et délicat. Il serait donc nécessaire d'en connaître les raisons.

Le développement durable étant un processus faisant appel à de nombreux acteurs qui subit des influences à des niveaux très divers (internationaux, régionaux, locaux), il est important d'aborder la question de l'intégration et de l'action que peuvent jouer les chercheurs universitaires à l'intérieur de ce système complexe.

> Quels sont les liens que doivent établir ces partenaires universitaires avec les autres acteurs? Qui peut jouer le rôle de médiation entre la recherche et son application? Le partenariat universitaire peut-il, par ses recherches, être un appui aux initiatives locales? Quels sont les modes de participation et de communication les plus appropriés pour que les fruits de la recherche soient mis aux bénéfices des populations locales? Voici quelques-unes des questions qui devraient être abordées au sein de ce groupe de travail.

Initiator: **Gerda Félay**, *AJPC, Lausanne*
Co-Moderators: **Mohammed Naciri**, *Université de Rabat, Maroc*
                        Jean-Marie Plancherel, *CFRC Coopération, EPFL Lausanne*
                        Jacques Dos Ghali, *CFRC Coopération, EPFL Lausanne*

Les discussions ont porté sur les thèmes suivants :

- ***Clarification conceptuelle***
  - le développement est autre chose qu'un simple transfert de ressources, de savoir-faire et de procédures
  - y a-t-il des formes d'intermédiation qui permettent de mettre en cohérence la nature initiale du projet et sa réalisation finale?

- ***Les représentations et l'intermédiation***
  - la transparence dans la gestion des projets ne signifie pas pour tous la même chose
  - savoir-faire et innovations technologiques nécessitent une modification des pratiques sociales
  - le partenariat se heurte aux inégalités grandissantes: sommes nous capables d'avoir des relations interpersonnelles et interculturelles allant dans le sens de la solidarité humaine?

- ***Le rôle des agents dans un processus d'intermédiation***
  - la problématique de l'intermédiation : quoi? comment? pour qui?
  - rôle ambigu du chercheur : à l'abri de pressions des décideurs politiques et le seul acteur engagé dans l'action disposé et motivé pour être à l'écoute des populations
  - favorise l'élaboration de la demande sociale, la fixation des priorités, et donc l'adhésion de la population au projet
  - les intermédiaires occupent des positions charnières et places stratégiques : partenaires motivants de la populations d'une part et en mesure de proposer des solutions alternatives mieux adaptées d'autre part

- influence positive sur les structures d'accueil de l'innovation

Points de vues divergents

Débat sur la nature du pouvoir: en effet, la représentation proposée des relations entre ces agents et les différents acteurs semble à plusieurs intervenants être marqué par une conception pyramidale classique des rapports de pouvoir.

Conclusions et propositions

Pour que l'intermédiation puisse être efficace, il faut lui assurer les conditions suivantes:
- considérer le *facteur temps* : essentiel pour la maturation, la réflexion et l'accumulation de savoirs et de pratiques
- placer l'intermédiation dans une *recherche-action* permet de prendre conscience de l'impact des réalisations et des actions propres de l'intervenant
- assurer le *calibrage des projets* en fonction des moyens et des capacités de prise en charge par les populations concernées;
- entreprendre *l'évaluation permanente* des objectifs, des modalités de gestion et des procédures appliquées
- promouvoir une *communication active*: faire apparaître les aspects positifs et négatifs sert d'outil de réflexion: la transparence fait le lien entre les buts et l'appropriation d'un projet par la population; l'autonomie favorise l'accumulation de savoir-faire.

compiled by Beat Sottas

Part IV   Annex

The Conference Participants - an Overview

The Conference was attended by 374 registered participants from 50 developing countries and 17 industrialised ones. About a quarter of the people attending the Conference (96) were from the South. More than 25% of the participants were women. There were 13 representatives of the media, and 9 members of the Conference staff.
The European continent dominated by far with 271 representatives, 72.4% of all the participants. Europe was followed by Africa with 53 representatives (14.2%), Asia with 28 representatives (7.4%), Latin America with 14 representatives (3.8%), and finally North America with 8 representatives (2.2%).
Thanks to the generous support of a number of sponsors (see p. 6) the Organising Committee was able to cover large part of the expenses of 72 invited participants, 57 of them from the South. The financial support was for travel, accommodation, per diems and registration fees. This help was given to 34 invited speakers and working-group moderators, and 38 other participants. Of the 15 representatives of the North receiving financial support, 10 were invited speakers or group-moderators.

Countries represented:

(in brackets are the number of representatives of the country concerned)

Argentina (1), Austria (4), Australia (1), Bangladesh (1), Belgium (3), Benin (1), Bhutan (1), Brazil (1), Burkina Faso (2), Burundi (1), Cameroon (1), Canada (2), Chad (1), Chile (2), Colombia (1), Costa Rica (2), Congo (1), Denmark (3), Egypt (2), El Salvador (1), Eritrea (2), France (13), Germany (5), Ghana (3), India (12), Indonesia (1), Iran (2), Ireland (1), Italy (2), Ivory Coast (2), Jordan (2), Kenya (7), Liechtenstein (1), Madagascar (1), Malawi (1), Malaysia (1), Mali (1), Mexico (1), Morocco (2), Netherlands (6), Niger (2), Nigeria (2), Norway (1), Pakistan (1), Paraguay (1), Peru (3), Philippines (2), Portugal (1), Senegal (4), Sierra Leone (1), Spain (1), South Africa (1), Sudan (2), Sweden (5), Switzerland (218), Tanzania (4), Thailand (1), Togo (1), Tunisia (1), Uganda (2), United Kingdom (7), USA (6), Venezuela (1), Vietnam (3), Zaire (2), Zambia (1), Zimbabwe (2)

Results of the evaluation questionnaire after the Conference

The questionnaire distributed at the end of the Conference was returned by 59 participants (30 from the North and 29 from the South), so the results are not fully representative. 57 of the respondents (about 96%) would like to have such a conference repeated (question 1).
The best interval of time in between this first and a possible second similar conference (question 2.1) was indicated as 2 to 3 years (about 75%). As for a possible location (question 2.2) 18 voted for an alternation between North and South and 18 for the South (61%) while only 12 representatives - about 20 % (3 of them from the South) - would prefer a repetition in the North.
The answers regarding the organisation that should be responsible for such a second conference were quite inhomogeneous: 12 voted for KFPE, 10 for a regional NGO in the South and 9 each for the South Center and for UN-bodies or specialised agencies.
As possible topics (question 2.4) a wide range of answers were given: follow-up on the same topic (13), capacity building in research (7), sustainable development (5), priority definition and research agendas (both 4) were the most frequent proposals.
Finally quite a lot of suggestions (question 3) were made: for example to present the results of the Conference soon (9), to build up databases and networks (5), to make "stock exchanges" for Research and Development projects (4), to prepare a smaller, more concentrated conference and to include industry, business and more NGOs (4), to organize small meetings before and after such a conference for better preparation and follow-up (3), and to identify common problems (3).

compiled by Daniel Maselli & Cornelia Zinsmeister

List and Addresses of Participants
(Countries in brackets indicate the original nationality)

Abdulai Awudu (Ghana)
Swiss Federal Institute of Technology
Department of Agriculture Economics
ETH Zentrum
Sonneggstrasse 33
CH-8092 Zürich Switzerland
Tel. +41 1 632 53 28
Fax: +41 1 632 10 86
e-mail: abdulai@iaw.agrl.ethz.ch

Aebischer Bernard
Energy Analysis Research Group
ETH Zentrum (ETL)
CH-8092 Zürich Switzerland
Tel. +41 1 632 41 95
Fax: +41 1 632 10 50
e-mail: bernard.aebischer@eeh.ee.ethz.ch

Aeschlimann André
Schweizerischer Nationalfonds (SNF)
Wildhainweg 20
CH-3001 Bern Switzerland
Tel. +41 31 308 22 22
Fax: +41 31 301 30 09

Afan Mawuto (Togo)
Faculté de théologie
Université de Fribourg
Miséricorde
CH-1700 Fribourg Switzerland
Tel. +41 37 86 68 11
Fax: +41 37 86 68 99

Agustoni-Phan Nhung (Vietnam)
Development & Environmental Management
Rehweg 4
CH-8044 Zürich Switzerland
Tel. & Fax: +41 1 820 23 64

Mohamed Aiai (Morocco)
Ingénieurs du Monde EPFL
Centre-midi EPF Lausanne
CH-1015 Ecublens Switzerland
Tel. +41 21 693 20 45

Alhassan Walter S.
Council for Scientific and
Industrial Research
P.O. Box M.32
Accra Ghana
Tel. +233 21 77 47 72
Fax: +233 21 77 76 55

Allende Jorge E.
Facultad de Medicina (Norte)
Universidad de Chile
Casilla 70086
Santiago 7 Chile
Tel. & Fax: +56 2 737 63 20
e-mail: jallende@abello.seci.uchile.cl

Alloush N. M. Said
Royal Scientific Society
P.O. Box 925819
Amman Jordan
Tel. +962 6 84 47 01
Fax: +962 6 84 48 06

Ammann Andreas
Calcutta Projekt Basel
Kantonsspital Basel
CH-4031 Basel Switzerland
Tel. & Fax. +41 61 265 22 01

Arhin Dyna Carol (Ghana)
London School of Hygiene &
Tropical Medicine
Keppel Street
WC1E 7HT London United Kingdom
Tel. +44 171 927 22 62
Fax: +44 171 637 53 91
e-mail: d.arhin@2shtm.ac.uk

Atteslander Peter
Swiss Institute for Development (SID)
Bözingenstrasse 71
CH-2502 Biel Switzerland
Tel. +41 32 52 30 50
Fax: +41 32 41 08 10
e-mail: sid@dial.eunet.ch

Augenbraun Eliene
USAID / PPC / ARC
Bureau for Policy and Program Coordination
Washington D.C. 20523 USA
Tel. +1 202 647 94 23
Fax: +1 202 647 85 95
e-mail: eaugenbraun@usaid.gov

Auroi Claude
Institut Universitaire d'Etudes
du Développement (IUED)
24, rue Rothschild, C.P. 136
CH-1211 Genève 21 Switzerland
Tel. +41 22 906 59 40
Fax: +41 22 906 59 47

Part IV
List and Addresses of Participants

Bâ Amadou Tidiane
Institut des sciences de l'environnement
Faculté des Sciences
Université Cheikh Anta Diop
B.P. 5005
Dakar Senegal
Tel. +221 24 23 02
Fax: +221 24 37 14
e-mail: ise@endadok.gn.apc.org

Bächler Günther
Swiss Peace Foundation
Wasserwerkgasse 7
Postfach 75
CH-3000 Bern 13 Switzerland
Tel. +41 31 311 55 82 / Fax: ... 83

Balaban Miriam (USA)
International Federation of Science Editors
School for Scientific Communication
Mario Negri Sud
I-66030 Santa Mario Imbaro Italy
Tel. +39 872 57 03 16 / Fax: ... 17
e-mail: balaban@cmns.mnegri.it

Balasubramanian Kothandaraman
M.S. Swaminathan Research Foundation
3rd Cross, Taramani Institutional Area
Madras 600 113 India
Tel. +91 44 235 12 29
Fax: +91 44 235 13 19
e-mail:
mssrf.madras@sm8.sprintrpg.sprint.com

Balegamire Bazilashe Juvenal (Zaire)
Sciences de l'Education
Université de Neuchâtel
Espace Louis-Agassiz 1
CH-2000 Neuchâtel Switzerland
Tel. +41 38 20 86 06
Fax: +41 38 21 37 60

Bangura Yusuf (Sierra Leone)
UNRISD
Palais des Nations
CH-1211 Genève 10 Switzerland
Tel. +41 22 798 84 00
Fax: +41 22 740 07 91

Barbey René
Institut Universitaire d'Etudes
du Développement (IUED)
24, rue Rothschild, C.P. 136
CH-1211 Genève 21 Switzerland
Tel. +41 22 906 59 97
Fax: +41 22 906 59 47

Barrow Robert O.
Federal Ministry of Science & Technology
New Federal Secretariat
Abuja Nigeria
Tel. +234 9 523 52 06
Fax: +234 9 523 52 04

Baumgartner Rudolf
Postgraduate Course on Developing
Countries (NADEL), ETH Zentrum
Rämistrasse 101
CH-8092 Zürich Switzerland
Tel. +41 1 632 50 98
Fax: +41 1 632 12 07

Bearth Thomas
Seminar für allgemeine
Sprachwissenschaft
Abteilung Afrikanistik
Universität Zürich
Plattenstrasse 54
CH-8032 Zürich Switzerland
Tel. +41 1 257 20 91
Fax: +41 1 980 41 81
e-mail: bearth@spw.unizh.ch

Bellwald Stefan
Center for Security Studies and
Conflict Research
ETH Zürich Zentrum
Scheuchzerstrasse 20
CH-8092 Zürich Switzerland
Tel. +41 1 632 40 25
Fax: +41 1 363 91 96
e-mail: stefch@hist.unizh.ch

Bender Heinz
Institut für Kulturtechnik
ETH Hönggerberg
CH-8093 Zürich Switzerland
Tel. +41 1 633 25 27
Fax: +41 1 633 10 84
e-mail: bender@ifk.baum.ethz.ch

Bernet Thomas
Institut für Agrarwirtschaft
ETH Zürich
Sonneggstrasse 33
CH-8092 Zürich Switzerland
Tel. +41 1 632 53 20
Fax: +41 1 632 10 86
e-mail: thomas.bernet@iaw.agrl.ethz.ch

Part IV   List and Addresses of Participants

Bertoni Siemens
Ministerio de Agricultura y Ganaderia
Sub-Secretariado de Estado de Recursos
Naturales y Medio Ambiente
Tacuary Nr. 443 - 4to. piso
Asuncion Paraguay
Tel. +595 21 44 35 54 / Fax: ... 01 67

Betschart Bruno
Institut de Zoologie
Université de Neuchâtel
11, rue Emile-Argand, C.P. 2
CH-2007 Neuchâtel Switzerland
Tel. +41 38 23 30 45 / Fax: ... 01
e-mail: bruno.betschart@uni.ne.ch

Betsche Peter F.
Seegüetli
CH-3800 Sundlauenen Switzerland
Tel. & Fax: +41 36 41 11 08

Beye Gora (Senegal)
Food and Agriculture Organization
of the United Nations (FAO)
Via delle Terme di Caracalla
I-00100 Roma Italy
Tel. +39 6 52 25 30 37
Fax: +39 6 52 25 57 31
e-mail: gora.beye.@fao.org

Bidaux Alain
Alter Ego / Urbaplan
21, avenue Montchoisi, C.P. 151
CH-1000 Lausanne Switzerland
Tel. +41 21 616 66 66
Fax: +41 21 616 41 31

Bitter Peter
Institute of Geography
University Zürich-Irchel
Winterthurerstrasse 190
CH-8057 Zürich Switzerland
Tel. +41 1 257 52 48
Fax: +41 1 362 52 27
e-mail: lanka@rsl.geogr.unizh.ch

Björnsen Astrid
Eibenstrasse 15
CH-8472 Winterthur Switzerland
Tel. +41 52 53 23 90
e-mail: bjoernsen@umnw.ethz.ch

Boissard Laurent
Montheolo 12 A
CH-1870 Monthey Switzerland
Tel. +41 25 71 40 97

Bolay Jean-Claude
IREC, EPF Lausanne
14, avenue de l'église anglaise
C.P. 555
CH-1006 Lausanne Switzerland
Tel. +41 21 693 62 13
Fax: +41 21 693 38 40
e-mail: bolay@dasun1.epfl.ch

Bonte-Friedheim Christian H. (Germany)
International Service for National
Agricultural Research (ISNAR)
P.O. Box 93375
NL-2509 AJ The Hague The Netherlands
Tel. +31 70 329 62 06
Fax: +31 70 381 96 77
e-mail: c.bonte-friedheim@cgnet.com

Bossart Rita
Hohlweg 1
CH-4125 Riehen Switzerland
Tel. +41 61 641 18 34

Bouldin Bill
Institut d'architecture
Université de Genève
Case Postale
CH-1200 Genève Switzerland
Tel. +41 22 735 58 80
Fax: +41 22 735 58 10
e-mail: bouldin@uni2a.unige.ch

Boulé Fabrice
Info Sud
Agence de Presse
10, chemin des Epinettes
CH-1007 Lausanne Switzerland
Tel. +41 21 617 43 53
Fax: +41 21 617 43 52
e-mail: infosud@fastnet.ch

Brun Reto
Swiss Tropical Institute (STI)
Socinstrasse 57, P.O. Box
CH-4002 Basel Switzerland
Tel. +41 61 284 82 31
Fax: +41 61 271 86 54

Brunner Martin
Ingenieurschule Rapperswil
Institut für Umwelttechnik
Oberseestrasse 10
CH-8640 Rapperswil Switzerland
Tel. +41 89 404 15 88
Fax: +41 55 23 44 00

Part IV — List and Addresses of Participants

Brunner Ursula
Expertengruppe SPPU
Grüngasse 31
CH-8004 Zürich Switzerland
Tel. +41 1 241 66 88
Fax: +41 1 242 91 58

Büchler Bettina
Scheuermattweg 6
CH-3007 Bern Switzerland
Tel. +41 31 371 98 62
e-mail: saebi@ubeclu.unibe.ch

Buess Marcus C.
Basel Mission
Library / Resource Centre
Missionsstrasse 21A
CH-4003 Basel Switzerland
Tel. +41 61 268 82 41 / Fax: ... 68

Bugenyi Frederick W.B.
National Agricultural Research Organization (NARO)
Fisheries Research Institute (FIRI)
P.O. Box 343
Jinja Uganda
Tel. +256 43 2 20 71
Fax: +256 43 2 17 27

Bührer Tobias
Loorenstrasse 74
CH-8053 Zürich Switzerland
Tel. +41 1 463 94 11
Fax: +41 1 462 33 65

Bui Thi Lang
Environmental Committee of Ho Chi Minh City
Bo Mon Rung Sac
79 Truong Dinh Street, District 1
Ho Chi Minh City Vietnam
Tel. +848 829 70 01
Fax: +848 896 15 12

Bustamante Alberto
Universitad Catolica de Peru
Canaval y Moreyra 454 - Piso 5
San Isidro
Lima Peru
Tel. +51 1 22 12 861
Fax: +51 1 42 16 729

Büttiker Willi
Lanzenbergstrasse 21
CH-4312 Magden Switzerland
Tel. & Fax: +41 61 841 16 04

Camacho Maria Antonieta
Escuela de Planificacion
Universidad Nacional
"Campus Omar Dengo"
Apdo-1-3011 Bawa
Heredia Costa Rica
Tel. +506 237 42 64
Fax: +506 237 70 32
e-mail: acamacho@irazu.una.ac.cr

Camenzind Jörg
Vereinigung für freies Unternehmertum (VfU)
Poststrasse 36
CH-7000 Chur Switzerland
Tel. +41 81 23 70 13
Fax: +41 81 23 70 27

Carl Klaus
International Institute of Biological Control, European Station
1, chemin des Grillons
CH-2800 Delémont Switzerland
Tel. +41 66 22 12 57
Fax: +41 66 20 05 15
e-mail: k.carl@cabi.org

Carlman Rolf
Department for Research Cooperation
SAREC / Sida
S-10525 Stockholm Sweden
Tel. +46 8 698 51 00 / Fax: ... 56 56
e-mail: rolf.carlman@sida.se

Carr Frances E.
USAID / PPC / RM 3889
320 21st Street NW
Washington D.C. 20523 USA
Tel. +1 202 647 70 59
Fax: +1 202 647 85 95
e-mail: fcarr@usaid.gov

Carstens Deon
Agricultural Councillor Embassy
59, Quai d'Orsay
F-75343 Paris France
Tel. +33 1 45 55 92 37
Fax: +33 1 45 51 76 54
e-mail: 100435.1431@compuserve.com

Castillo Gelia T.
International Rice Research Institute (IRRI)
P.O. Box 933
1099 Manila Philippines
Tel. +63 94 5 13 93
Fax: +63 2 891 12 92

Part IV List and Addresses of Participants

Cerutti Fabio
Federal Office for Agriculture
Mattenhofstrasse 5
CH-3006 Bern Switzerland
Tel. +41 31 322 59 50 / Fax: ... 26 34
e-mail: fabio.cerutti@blw.admin.ch

Cetto Ana Maria
UNAM Instituto de Fisica
Dept. de Fisica Teorica
A.P. 20-364
01000 México D.F. Mexico
Tel. +525 622 51 52
Fax: +525 622 5015
e-mail: ana@sysul1.ifisicacu.unam.mx

Charmes Jacques
Institut Français de Recherche
Scientifique pour le développement
en Coopération (ORSTOM)
Département Sud
213, rue La Fayette
F-75480 Paris Cedex 10 France
Tel. +33 1 48 03 77 77
Fax: +33 1 48 03 78 32
e-mail: charmes@paris.orstom.fr

Chatelain Cyrille
Conservatoire & Jardin botaniques
de la Ville de Genève
B.P. 60
CH-1292 Chambésy Switzerland
Tel. & Fax: +41 22 732 69 69
e-mail: chatelain@cjb.unige.ch

Chattoo Bharat B.
Departement of Microbiology &
Biotechnology Centre
University of Baroda
390 002 Baroda India
Tel. +91 265 32 77 96
Fax: +91 265 33 92 31
e-mail: bbc@bcmsu.ernet.in

Chebbi Camelia
Stöberstrasse 27
CH-4055 Basel Switzerland
Tel. +41 61 266 56 27

Chevallier Corinne
Institut Universitaire d'Etudes
du Développement (IUED)
24, rue Rothschild, C.P. 136
CH-1211 Genève 21 Switzerland
Tel. +41 22 906 59 40 / Fax: ... 47

Chhetri Ganesh B.
Royal Government of Bhutan
Ministry of Agriculture
P.O. Box 292
Thimphu Buthan
Tel. +975 29 30 02 09
Fax: +975 2 93 02

Chiffelle Frédéric
Institut de Géographie
Université de Neuchâtel
Espace Louis-Agassiz 1, B.P. 499
CH-2001 Neuchâtel Switzerland
Tel. +41 38 20 87 09
Fax: +41 38 21 37 60

Chimanikire Donald P.
Institute of Development Studies (IDS)
University of Zimbabwe
Mount Pleasant, P.O. Box MP. 167
Harare Zimbabwe
Tel. +263 4 33 33 41 / Fax: ... 45

Chiotha Sosten
University of Malawi
P.O. Box 278
Zomba Malawi
Tel. +265 52 26 22 / Fax: ... 27 60
e-mail: schiotha@unima.apc.wn.org

Chollet Martial
Intercoopération
Maulbeerstrasse 10
CH-3001 Bern Switzerland
Tel. +41 31 382 31 25 / Fax: ... 36 05

Cissé Gueladio
Ecole inter-états d'ingénieurs de
l'équipement rural (EIER)
B.P. 7023
Ouagadougou Burkina Faso
Tel. +226 30 71 16
Fax: +226 31 27 24

Clément Geneviève
80, rue de Meyrin
F-01210 Ferney-Voltaire France
Tel. +33 50 40 76 50

Clottu Vogel Anne-Christine
Swiss Academy of Sciences (SAS)
Bärenplatz 2
CH-3011 Bern Switzerland
Tel. +41 31 311 33 75
Fax: +41 31 312 32 91
e-mail: clottu@sanw.unibe.ch

Part IV — List and Addresses of Participants

Comby Bernard
National Councillor
Tovassière
CH-1907 Saxon Switzerland
Tel. & Fax: +41 26 44 12 66

Comeliau Christian (France)
Institut Universitaire d'Etudes
du Développement (IUED)
24, rue Rothschild, C.P. 136
CH-1211 Genève 21 Switzerland
Tel. +41 22 906 59 40
Fax: +41 22 906 59 47

Corminboeuf Christian
Institut Universitaire d'Etudes
du Développement (IUED)
24, rue Rothschild, C.P. 136
CH-1211 Genève 21 Switzerland
Tel. +41 22 906 59 40
Fax: +41 22 906 59 47
e-mail: corminbo@uni2a.unige.ch

Cotti Flavio
Federal Councillor
Department of Foreign Affairs
Bundeshaus West
CH-3003 Bern Switzerland
Tel. +41 31 322 21 11
Fax: +41 31 322 32 37

Davidsson Lena (Sweden)
Institute for Food Science
Laboratory for Human Nutrition
ETH Zürich
Seestrasse 72, P.O. Box 474
CH-8803 Rüschlikon Switzerland
Tel. +41 1 724 21 44
Fax: +41 1 724 01 83
e-mail: davidsson@ilw.agrl.ethz.ch

Debessay Dawit (Eritrea)
28, rue des grottes
CH-1201 Genève Switzerland
Tel. +41 22 734 62 30

De Munck Eric
European Centre for Development Policy
Management (ECDPM) / SADAOC
Onze Lieve Vrouweplein 21
NL-6211 HE Maastricht The Netherlands
Tel. +31 43 350 29 00
Fax: +31 43 350 29 02
e-mail: sadaoc@ecdpm.org

Del Vecchio Janina (Costa Rica)
Embassy of Costa Rica
Thunstrasse 150E
CH-3047 Bern Switzerland
Tel. +41 31 952 62 30
Fax: +41 31 952 64 57

Desarzens Claude
Maunoir 48
CH-1207 Genève Switzerland
Tel. & Fax: +41 22 700 13 15

De Sousa Reis Guadelupe
Vienna Institute for Development
and Cooperation (VIDC)
Weyergasse 5
A-1030 Wien Austria
Tel. +43 1 713 35 94 74
Fax: +43 1 713 35 94 73

Diouf Papa Ndiaye (Senegal)
Institut Universitaire d'Etudes
du Développement (IUED)
24, rue Rothschild, C.P. 136
CH-1211 Genève 21 Switzerland
Tel. +41 22 906 59 40
Fax: +41 22 906 59 47

Dolfini Marco
Swiss Institute of Development (SID)
Bözingenstrasse 71
CH-2502 Biel Switzerland
Tel. +41 32 52 30 50
Fax: +41 32 41 08 10
e-mail: sid@dial.eunet.ch

Dos Ghali Jacques
EPF Lausanne
CH-1015 Lausanne Switzerland
Tel. +41 21 693 26 36
Fax: +41 21 693 26 87
e-mail: jacques.dosghali@deqm.epfl.ch

Dossahoua Traore
University of Abidjan, FAST
P.O. Box 519
Abidjan 08 Ivory Coast
Tel. +225 31 75 64
Fax: +225 44 04 12

Drösler Matthias
Landscape Ecology
Ortsstrasse 23
D-85354 Freising Germany
Tel. & Fax: +49 8161 33 86

Part IV List and Addresses of Participants

Dubois Jean-Bernard
Swiss Agency for Development
and Cooperation (SDC)
Fachdienst Umwelt und Forstwirtschaft
Schwarztorstrasse 59
CH-3003 Bern Switzerland
Tel. +41 31 325 92 80
Fax: +41 31 325 93 62

Eade Deborah (United Kingdom)
Development in Practice
6, av. de Luzerna
CH-1203 Genève Switzerland
Tel. +41 22 344 03 88

Edelmann Claudia
Zürichbergstrasse 18
CH-8008 Zürich Switzerland
Tel. +41 1 632 05 51 / Fax: ... 10 45
e-mail: ede@bwi.eth.ch

Egger Paul
Swiss Agency for Development
and Cooperation (SDC)
Eigerstrasse 73
CH-3003 Bern Switzerland
Tel. +41 31 322 34 46 / Fax: ... 16 93
e-mail: paul.egger@sdc.admin.ch

Egger-Tschäppeler Ruth
Intercoopération (IC)
Maulbeerstrasse 10, P.O. Box 6724
CH-3001 Bern Switzerland
Tel. +41 31 382 08 61 / Fax: ... 36 05

Eggmann Betschart Cornelia
(Switzerland)
LRP / ASP; P.O. Box 144
Nanyuki Kenya
Tel. +254 176 325 27
Fax: +254 176 222 01
e-mail: lrp1@elci.gn.apc.org

Egwang Thomas Gordon
Med Biotech Laboratories (MBL)
P.O. Box 9364
Kampala Uganda
Tel. +256 41 268 251
Fax: +256 41 257 179

Ehrler Franz
Secrétariat ESKAS
1, route du Jura
CH-1700 Fribourg Switzerland
Tel. +41 37 26 74 24
Fax: +41 37 26 74 04

Eichholzer Erika
Linsebühlstrasse 9
CH-9000 St.Gallen Switzerland
Tel. & Fax: +41 71 22 08 60

EL-Fouly Mohamed Mostafa
National Research Center
Botany Department
EL-Tahrir Street
Cairo-Dokki Egypt
Tel. +202 336 12 30
Fax: +202 361 08 50

El-Nadi Lotfia (Egypt)
Qatar University
Faculty of Science
Physics Department
Doha Qatar
Tel. +974 89 21 78
Fax: +974 89 27 77

Favez Valérie
Agence Télégraphique Suisse SA (ATS)
Länggassstrasse 7
CH-3001 Berne Switzerland
Tel. +41 31 309 33 33
Fax: +41 31 301 85 38

Favrat Daniel
LENI-DGM, EPF Lausanne
CH-1015 Lausanne Switzerland
Tel. +41 21 693 25 11
Fax: +41 21 693 35 02
e-mail: daniel.favrat@it.dgm.epfl.ch

Federspiel Geneviève
Institute of Biotechnology
ETH Hönggerberg
CH-8093 Zürich Switzerland
Tel. +41 1 633 36 84
Fax: +41 1 633 10 76
e-mail: feder@biotech.biol.ethz.ch

Fellay Gerda
Association Jeunesse & Parents
Conseils (AJPC)
25, avenue L. Ruchonnet
CH-1003 Lausanne Switzerland
Tel. +41 21 312 83 55
Fax: +41 21 320 87 31

Ferrari Sergio
Correspondant pour l'Amérique latine
Rossfeldstrasse 40
CH-3004 Bern Switzerland
Tel. & Fax: +41 31 301 76 55

Fischer Felix
Bundesamt für Aussenwirtschaft (BAWI)
Entwicklungsdienst / Finanzsektion II
Effingerstrasse 1
CH-3003 Bern Switzerland
Tel. +41 31 324 08 18 / Fax: ... 09 62
e-mail: felix.fischer@bawi.admin.ch

Flury Manuel
Interdisciplinary Center for General Ecology
University of Berne
Falkenplatz 16
CH-3012 Bern Switzerland
Tel. +41 31 631 39 52 / Fax: ... 87 33
e-mail: flury@ikaoe.unibe.ch

Fogelberg Theresa
Directorate General for Development
Cooperation (DGIS)
Ministry of Foreign Affairs
P.O. Box 20061
NL-2500 EB The Hague The Netherlands
Tel. +31 70 348 60 34
Fax: +31 70 348 58 88

Forster Jacques
Institut Universitaire d'Etudes
du Développement (IUED)
24, rue Rothschild, C.P. 136
CH-1211 Genève 21 Switzerland
Tel. +41 22 906 59 40 / Fax: ... 47

Forster Willi G.
K. Winzeler & Partner AG
Fliederstrasse 16
CH-8006 Zürich Switzerland
Tel. +41 1 251 92 51
Fax: +41 1 261 09 61

Francisco Raquel V.
Philippine Atmospheric, Geophysical &
Astronomical Services Administration
(PAGASA)
1424 Quezon Avenue
Quezon City Philippines
Tel. +63 2 922 72 82
Fax: +63 2 922 78 13

Frey Joachim
Institute for Veterinary Bacteriology
University of Berne
Länggassstrasse 122
CH-3012 Bern Switzerland
Tel. +41 31 631 24 84
Fax: +41 31 631 26 34
e-mail: jfrfy@vbi.unibe.ch

Freymond Jean
Centre d'etudes pratiques de la
négociation internationale
11a, avenue de la Paix
CH-1202 Genève Switzerland
Tel. +41 22 734 89 50
Fax: +41 22 733 64 44

Freyvogel Thierry A.
Swiss Tropical Institute (STI)
Socinstrasse 57, P.O. Box
CH-4002 Basel Switzerland
Tel. +41 61 284 82 20
Fax: +41 61 271 86 54
e-mail: tanner@unbaclu.unibas.ch

Freyvogel-Jenni Nadine
Schützengraben 13
CH-4051 Basel Switzerland
Tel. +41 61 261 77 61

Friboulet Jean-Jacques
Séminaire de politique économique
et sociale (SPES)
Université de Fribourg, Miséricorde
CH-1700 Fribourg Switzerland
Tel. +41 37 29 82 18
Fax: +41 37 29 97 00

Frischknecht Kurt P.
Pädagogische Hochschule Kanton St. Gallen
Notkerstrasse 27
CH-9004 St.Gallen Switzerland
Tel. +41 71 243 94 20
Fax: +41 71 243 94 90

Fritsch Martin
Institut für Kulturtechnik
Fachbereich Wasser & Boden
ETH Hönggerberg
CH-8093 Zürich Switzerland
Tel. +41 1 633 29 99
Fax: +41 1 633 10 84
e-mail: fritsch@ifk.baum.ethz.ch

Fust Walter
Swiss Agency for Development
and Cooperation (SDC)
Eigerstrasse 73
CH-3003 Bern Switzerland
Tel. +41 31 322 34 01 / Fax: ... 35 05

Gabriel Natalie
Offenburgerstrasse 61
CH-4057 Basel Switzerland
Tel. +41 61 693 09 35

Part IV List and Addresses of Participants

Gaillard Jacques
ORSTOM, Centre de Bondy
72, route d'Aulnay
F-93143 Bondy Cedex France
Tel. +33 1 48 02 55 17
Fax: +33 1 48 47 30 88
e-mail: gaillard@bondy.orstom.fr

Galtung Johan
51, Bois Chatton
F-01210 Versonnex France
Tel. +33 50 42 73 06 / Fax: ... 75 06

Gapany Hélène
Université de Fribourg
CH-1702 Fribourg Switzerland
Tel. +41 37 29 82 18 / Fax: ... 97 00

Gautier Laurent
Conservatoire & Jardin botaniques
de la Ville de Genève
C.P. 60
CH-1292 Chambésy Switzerland
Tel. +41 22 732 69 69
Fax: +41 22 738 45 97
e-mail: gautier@cjb.unige.ch

Gebremedhin Naigzy
Eritrean Agency for Environment (EAE)
P.O. Box 5713
Asmara Eritrea
Tel. +291 1 18 10 77 / Fax: ... 14 16
e-mail: eae@er.punchdown.org

Geiser Urs
Institute of Geography
University of Zürich-Irchel
Winterthurerstrasse 190
CH-8057 Zürich Switzerland
Tel. +41 1 257 51 65
Fax: +41 1 362 52 27
e-mail: ugeiser@rsl.geogr.unizh.ch

Georgi Andrea
Offenburgerstrasse 61
CH-4057 Basel Switzerland
Tel. +41 61 693 09 35

Gerber Brigitta
Swiss Agency for Development
and Cooperation (SDC)
Policy and Research Section
Eigerstrasse 73
CH-3003 Bern Switzerland
Tel. +41 31 322 34 63 / Fax: ... 324 16 92
e-mail: brigitta.gerber@sdc.admin.ch

Germann Thomas
Vogelsangweg 5
CH-4410 Liestal Switzerland
Tel. +41 61 921 29 79

Germann-Meyer Vreni
Tiergarten-Gesellschaft Zürich
Klosbachstrasse 150
CH-8032 Zürich Switzerland
Tel. & Fax: +41 1 251 95 02

Gern Lise
Institut de zoologie
11, rue Emile-Argand
CH-2000 Neuchâtel Switzerland
Tel. +41 38 23 30 52
Fax: +41 38 23 30 01
e-mail: lise.gern@zool.unine.ch

Gerster Richard
Swiss Coalition of Development
Organizations
Monbijoustrasse 31, P.O. Box 6735
CH-3001 Bern Switzerland
Tel. +41 31 381 17 11
Fax: +41 31 381 17 18
e-mail: scoalition@igc.apc.org

Gfeller Elisabeth
9, rue Vaucher
CH-2000 Neuchâtel Switzerland

Gichuki Francis Ndegwa
Soil and Water Management Programme
Department of Agricultural Engineering
University of Nairobi
P.O. Box 30197
Nairobi Kenya
Tel. +254 2 63 17 93
Fax: +254 2 59 34 65
e-mail: swmp@ken.healthnet.org

Giovannini Jean-François
Swiss Agency for Development
and Cooperation (SDC)
Eigerstrasse 73
CH-3003 Bern Switzerland
Tel. +41 31 322 34 23
Fax: +41 31 324 16 91

Gonzalez Jose M.
Ecology and Close-loop Economy Group
Calle 80 no B-84
Bogotà Colombia
Tel. +571 211 33 27 / Fax: ... 11 54
e-mail: rgomez@colomsat.net.co

Part IV List and Addresses of Participants

Grass Alexander
Radio DRS, Auslandredaktion
Schwarztorstrasse 21, P.O. Box
CH-3007 Bern Switzerland
Tel. +41 31 388 91 11
Fax: +41 31 388 95 20

Grossenbacher Walter
Swiss Priority Programm
Environment (SPPE)
Länggassstrasse 23
CH-3012 Bern Switzerland
Tel. +41 31 302 55 77
Fax: +41 31 302 55 20
e-mail: ppemod@cumuli.vmsmail.ethz.ch

Guala Florence
Institut Universitaire d'Etudes
du Développement (IUED)
24, rue Rothschild, C.P. 136
CH-1211 Genève 21 Switzerland
Tel. +41 22 906 59 40
Fax: +41 22 906 59 47

Guinko Sita
Université Ougadougou
Ouagadougou Burkina Faso
Tel. +226 30 70 64
Fax: +226 30 72 42

Häberli Rudolf
Swiss Priority Programm
Environment (SPPE)
Länggassstrasse 23
CH-3012 Bern Switzerland
Tel. +41 31 302 55 77
Fax: +41 31 302 55 20
e-mail: ppemod@cumuli.vmsmail.ethz.ch

Hadorn Adrian
Swiss Agency for Development
and Cooperation (SDC)
Policy and Research Section
Eigerstrasse 73
CH-3003 Bern Switzerland
Tel. +41 31 322 34 51
Fax: +41 31 324 16 92
e-mail: adrian.hadorn@sdc.admin.ch

Haller René D. (Switzerland)
Baobab Farm Ltd.
P.O. Box 81995
Mombasa Kenya
Tel. +254 11 48 61 55
Fax: +254 11 48 61 57

Hammer Thomas
Poudrière 17
CH-1700 Fribourg Switzerland
Tel. +41 37 24 01 77

Hardie John
International Development Research
Centre (IDRC)
P.O. Box 8500
Ottawa Ontario Canada K1G 3H9
Tel. +1 613 236 61 63
Fax: +1 613 235 63 91
e-mail: jhardie@idrc.ca

Hassan Mohamed Hag Ali (Sudan)
Third World Academy of Science (TWAS)
Miramare, Strada Costiera 11
P.O. Box 586
I-34100 Trieste Italy
Tel. +39 40 22 401
Fax: +39 40 22 41 63
e-mail: twas@ictp.trieste.it

Hassan Seif (Sudan)
Habitat Group Department for Architecture
ETH Zürich Hönggerberg
Postfach H45.2
CH-8093 Zürich Switzerland
Tel. +41 1 633 29 75
Fax: +41 1 633 10 63

Hauck Bernard
Swiss Academy of Sciences (SAS)
Bärenplatz 2
CH-3011 Bern Switzerland
Tel. +41 31 311 33 75
Fax: +41 31 312 32 91
e-mail: hauck@iastro.unil.ch

Haug Anette
The Research Council of Norway
Stensberggata 26, P.O. Box 2700
N-0131 Oslo Norway
Tel. +47 22 03 70 00
Fax: +47 22 03 70 01
e-mail: anette.haug@nfr.no

Heim Thomas
Nachdiplomstudium Umwelt
Ingenieurschule Muttenz
Gründenstrasse 40
CH-4132 Muttenz Switzerland
Tel. +41 61 46 74 259
Fax: +41 61 46 74 460

Part IV   List and Addresses of Participants

Herren Urs
Swiss Agency for Development
and Cooperation (SDC)
Policy and Research Section
Eigerstrasse 73
CH-3003 Bern Switzerland
Tel. +41 31 322 34 39
Fax: +41 31 324 16 92
e-mail: urs.herren@sdc.admin.ch

Hicks Esther
Faculty of Management and Organization
Noorderkerkstraat 3, P.O. Box 80
NL-09700 AV Groningen The Netherlands
Tel. +31 50 36 33 482
Fax: +31 50 31 31 747
e-mail: e.k.hicks@bdk.rug.nl

Hjorth Peder
Department Water Resources Eng.
Lund University
P.O. Box 118
S-22100 Lund Sweden
Tel. +46 46 222 48 71 / Fax: ... 44 35
e-mail: peder.hjorth@tvrl.lth.se

Högger Ruedi
Ringstrasse 9
CH-3066 Stettlen Switzerland
Tel. +41 31 931 43 51

Hohl Hans R.
Institute for Plantbiology
University of Zürich
Zollikerstrasse 107
CH-8008 Zürich Switzerland
Tel. +41 1 385 42 11 / Fax: ... 04
e-mail: hohl@botinst.unizh.ch

Hornstein Pius
Theodorsgraben 40
CH-4058 Basel Switzerland
Tel. +41 61 691 37 10
Fax: +41 61 681 20 54

Hossain Talim
Alpha Consults Ltd.
45, Sonargaon Road
Dhaka 1205 Bangladesh
Tel. +880 2 38 09 41

Hountondji Paulin J.
Department of Philosophy
National University of Benin
B.P. 1268
Cotonou Benin

Tel. +229 33 00 02
Fax: +229 33 25 49

Howell John
Overseas Development Institute (ODI)
Regent's College, Inner Circle
Regent's Park
London NW1 4NS United Kingdom
Tel. +44 171 487 74 13
Fax: +44 171 487 75 90
e-mail: director@odi.org.uk

Hufty Marc (Canada)
Institut Universitaire d'Etudes
du Développement (IUED)
24, rue Rothschild, C.P. 136
CH-1211 Genève 21 Switzerland
Tel. +41 22 906 59 65
Fax: +41 22 906 59 47
e-mail: hufty@uni2a.unige.ch

Hurtado Pozo José (Peru)
Séminaire de droit pénal
Université de Fribourg, Miséricorde
CH-1700 Fribourg Switzerland
Tel. +41 37 29 80 71
Fax: +41 37 29 97 51
e-mail: jose.-hurtado@unifr.ch

Ilangumaran Suburaj (Indonesia)
Indo-Swiss Collaboration in Biotechnology
Institute of Biotechnology
ETH Hönggerberg
CH-8093 Zürich Switzerland
Tel. +41 1 633 21 95
Fax: +41 1 633 10 76
e-mail: jenny@biotech.biol.ethz.ch

Jain Randhir B.
Department of Political Science
University of Delhi
38/18 Probyn Road
Delhi 110007 India
Tel. & Fax: +91 11 725 74 72

Jaubert Ronald (France)
Institut Universitaire d'Etudes
du Développement (IUED)
24, rue Rothschild, C.P. 136
CH-1211 Genève 21 Switzerland
Tel. +41 22 906 59 40
Fax: +41 22 906 59 47
e-mail: jaubert.@uni2a.unibe.ch

Part IV   List and Addresses of Participants

Jayaraman Kunthala
Centre for Biotechnology
Anna University Madras
600025 Guiniy India
Tel. & Fax: +91 44 235 02 99

Jenkins Jennifer (United Kingdom)
Swiss Tropical Institute (STI)
Socinstrasse 57, P.O. Box
CH-4002 Basel Switzerland
Tel. +41 61 284 84 28
Fax: +41 61 271 79 51

Jenkins Paul (United Kingdom)
Basler Mission Archive
CH-4003 Basel Switzerland
Tel. +41 61 268 82 45 / Fax: ... 68

Jenny Katharina
Institute for Biotechnology
ETH-Hönggerberg
CH-8093 Zürich Switzerland
Tel. +41 1 633 21 95
Fax: +41 1 633 10 76
e-mail: jenny@biotech.biol.ethz.ch

Jung Roger A. U.
Ecole d'ingénieurs du Canton de
Neuchâtel (EICN)
7, Hôtel-de-Ville
CH-2400 Le Locle Switzerland
Tel. +41 39 34 12 12
Fax: +41 39 31 26 07

Kapaga Angolwisye M.
Animal Disease Research Institute
(ADRI), Pathology Department
P.O. Box 9254
Dar-es-Salaam Tanzania
Tel. & Fax: +255 51 86 31 04

Kappel Rolf
Postgraduate Course on Developing
Countries (NADEL), ETH Zentrum
Rämistrasse 101
CH-8092 Zürich Switzerland
Tel. +41 1 632 42 40
Fax: +41 1 632 12 07

Käppeli Othmar
Agency for Biosafety Research (BATS)
Clarastrasse 13
CH-4058 Basel Switzerland
Tel. +41 61 690 93 10
Fax: +41 61 690 93 15
e-mail: kaeppeli@ubaclu.unibas.ch

Kaufmann Christian
Museum für Völkerkunde Basel
Augustinergasse 2
CH-4001 Basel Switzerland
Tel. +41 61 266 56 70
Fax: +41 61 266 56 05

Keller Roland
Institut de botanique
Université de Lausanne
CH-1015 Lausanne Switzerland
Tel. +41 21 692 42 69
Fax: +41 21 692 41 05
e-mail: roland.keller@ibsg.unil.ch

Khor Kok Peng Martin
Third World Network (TWN)
228 Macalister Road
10400 Penang Malaysia
Tel. +60 4 226 67 28
Fax: +60 4 226 45 05
e-mail: twn@igc.apc.org

King'oriah George Kinoti
Egerton University
P.O. Box 536
Njoro Kenya
Tel. +254 37 61 620
Fax: +254 37 61 405

Kitua Andrew Yona (Tanzania)
Ifakara Centre
c/o Swiss Tropical Institute (STI)
Socinstrasse 57, P.O. Box
CH-4002 Basel Switzerland
Tel. +41 61 284 82 83
Fax: +41 61 271 79 51

Kohn Michael
Arbeitskreis Kapital und
Wirtschaft
Postfach 4813
CH-8022 Zürich Switzerland
Tel. +41 1 281 16 16
Fax: +41 1 202 92 83

Korte Rolf
Deutsche Gesellschaft für technische
Zusammenarbeit (GTZ) GmbH
Dag Hammarskjöld Weg 1
Postfach 5180
D-63536 Eschborn Germany
Tel. +49 6196 79 12 24
Fax: +49 6196 79 71 04

Part IV List and Addresses of Participants

Krauer Jürg
Group for Development &
Environment (GfEU)
University of Berne
Hallerstrasse 12
CH-3012 Bern Switzerland
Tel. +41 31 631 37 53
Fax: +41 31 631 85 44

Kristensen Thomas K.
Danish Bilharziasis Laboratory
Jaegersborg Allé 1
DK-2920 Charlottenlund Denmark
Tel. +45 39 62 61 68
Fax: +45 31 62 61 21
e-mail: biladblp@pop.denet.dk

Küchler Felix A.
Swiss Tropical Institute (STI)
Socinstrasse 57, P.O. Box
CH-4002 Basel Switzerland
Tel. +41 61 284 84 34
Fax: +41 61 271 79 51

Künzi Erwin (Switzerland)
LRP/ASP
P.O. Box 144
Nanyuki Kenya
Tel. +254 176 32 5 27
Fax: +254 176 222 01
e-mail: lrp@elci.gn.apc.org

Langenegger Otto
Interkantonale Ingenieurschule St. Gallen
Rösslistrasse 23
CH-9056 Gais Switzerland
Tel. & Fax: +41 71 93 27 48
e-mail: otto.langenegger@isg.ch

Larcher Marie-Therese
Free Lance Journalist
Haldenstrasse 16
CH-8142 Uitikon Switzerland
Tel. & Fax: +41 1 491 61 16

Lassonde Louise
Fondation du Devenir, C.P. 2720
CH-1211 Genève 2 Switzerland
Tel. +41 22 705 81 76
Fax: +41 22 734 85 52

Läuffer Peter
Schweizer Fernsehen DRS
CH-3000 Bern 14 Switzerland
Tel. +41 31 388 91 11
Fax: +41 31 388 95 20

Laurent François
Alter Ego / Urbaplan
21, avenue de Montchiri 21, C.P. 151
CH-1000 Lausanne 19 Switzerland
Tel. +41 21 616 66 66
Fax: +41 21 616 41 31

Leisinger Klaus
Ciba-Geigy Foundation for Cooperation
with Developing Countries
Klybeckstrasse 141, P.O. Box
CH-4002 Basel Switzerland
Tel. +41 61 696 13 17
Fax: +41 61 696 22 39

Lele Uma (India)
The World Bank Group
ESDAR/S7-043
1818 H Street N.W.
Washington D.C. 20433 United States
Tel. +1 202 473 06 19
Fax: +1 202 522 32 46
e-mail: ulele@worldbank.org

Lengeler Christian
Swiss Tropical Institute (STI)
Socinstrasse 57, P.O. Box
CH-4051 Basel Switzerland
Tel. +41 61 284 82 21
Fax: +41 61 271 79 51
e-mail: lengeler@ubaclu.unibas.ch

Lenhard Vera
Greenpeace Switzerland
Müllerstrasse 37
CH-8026 Zürich Switzerland
Tel. +41 1 295 94 27
Fax: +41 1 241 38 21

Leuenberger Heinz
Ingenieurschule beider Basel
Gründenstrasse 40
CH-4132 Muttenz Switzerland
Tel. +41 61 467 43 12
Fax: +41 61 467 44 60
e-mail: leu@ibb.ch

Leuenberger Alexander
PORT
CH-3655 Sigriswil Switzerland
Tel. +41 31 631 85 42
Fax: +41 33 51 27 26
e-mail: alex@klimet.unibe.ch

Part IV — List and Addresses of Participants

Leuthold Margrit
ETH Zürich HG J 65
Präsidialstrasse 3
CH-8092 Zürich Switzerland
Tel. +41 1 632 58 99
Fax: +41 1 632 11 52
e-mail: leuthold@sl.ethz.ch

Lindt Meinrad
Biozentrum der Universität Basel
Abteilung Biochemie
Klingelbergstrasse 70
CH-4056 Basel Switzerland
Tel. +41 61 267 21 66
Fax: +41 61 267 21 09
e-mail: lindt.@urz.unibas.ch

Liniger Hanspeter
Group for Development &
Environment (GfEU)
University of Berne
Hallerstrasse 12
CH-3012 Bern Switzerland
Tel. +41 31 631 88 22
Fax: +41 31 631 85 44
e-mail: liniger@giub.unibe.ch

Lobos Edgar (El Salvador)
Swiss Tropical Institute (STI)
Socinstrasse 57, P.O. Box
CH-4002 Basel Switzerland
Tel. +41 61 284 82 47
Fax: +41 61 271 86 54

Lorenz Nicolaus
Swiss Tropical Institute (STI) &
Medicus Mundi
Socinstrasse 57, P.O. Box
CH-4002 Basel Switzerland
Tel. +41 61 284 82 20
Fax: +41 61 271 86 54

Loutan Louis C.
Unité de médecine communautaire
Policlinique de médecine (HCUG)
34, rue Micheli-du-Cres
CH-1211 Genève Switzerland
Tel. +41 22 372 96 10
Fax: +41 22 372 96 26

Löw Catherine
Calcutta Project Basel
Kantonsspital Basel
CH-4031 Basel Switzerland
Tel. & Fax: +41 61 265 22 01

Luisoni Emilio
Institut Universitaire d'Etude
du Développement (IUED)
24, rue Rothschild, C.P. 136
CH-1211 Genève 21 Switzerland
Tel. +41 22 906 59 40
Fax: +41 22 906 59 47

Lumbiarres Beatrice
FUNDES
Hauptstrasse 10, P.O. Box
CH-8872 Weesen Switzerland
Tel. +41 58 43 66 50 / Fax: ... 51

Lundgren Björn
International Foundation for Science
IFS
Grev Turegatan 19
S-114 38 Stockholm Sweden
Tel. +46 8 545 818 21 / Fax: ... 01
e-mail: blu@ifs.se

Lys Jon-Andri
Müllheimstrasse 48
CH-4057 Basel Switzerland
Tel. +41 61 693 13 66

Maillefer Etienne
Université de Neuchâtel / CRD
Pierre-à-Nazel 7
CH-2000 Neuchâtel Switzerland
Tel. +41 38 21 10 85

Maina Francisca
DURP
University of Nairobi
P.O. Box 51822
Nairobi Kenya
Tel. +254 234 09 72
Fax: +254 271 85 48
e-mail: lrp@elci.gn.apc.org

Marmet David
Engehaldenstrasse 57
CH-3012 Bern Switzerland
Tel. +41 31 302 37 21

Maselli Daniel
Swiss Commission for Research
Partnership with Developing Countries
(KFPE)
Bärenplatz 2
CH-3011 Bern Switzerland
Tel. +41 31 311 06 01
Fax: +41 31 312 16 78 / ...32 91
e-mail: maselli@sanw.unibe.ch

Part IV   List and Addresses of Participants

Materu Peter Nicolas
Faculty of Engineering
University of Dar-es-Salaam
P.O. Box 35131
Dar-es-Salaam Tanzania
Tel. +255 51 43 753 / Fax: ... 376
e-mail: materu@unidar.gn.apc.org

Mathur Eva
Clinic of Infertility and Gynaecological Endocrinology
Geneva University Hospital
20, rue Alide-Jentzer
CH-1211 Genève Switzerland
Tel. +41 22 382 43 42 / Fax: ... 13

Mathys Renata
Institute for Biotechnology
ETH Hönggerberg
CH-8093 Zürich Switzerland
Tel. +41 1 633 36 90
Fax: +41 1 633 10 51
e-mail: mathys@biotech.biol.ethz.ch

Maurer Jean-Luc
Institut Universitaire d'Etudes
du Développement (IUED)
24, rue Rothschild, C.P. 136
CH-1211 Genève 21 Switzerland
Tel. +41 22 906 59 40
Fax: +41 22 906 59 47
e-mail: maurer@uni2a.unige.ch

Mäusezahl Daniel
Swiss Tropical Institute (STI)
Socinstrasse 57, P.O. Box
CH-4002 Basel Switzerland
Tel. +41 61 284 84 29
Fax: +41 61 271 79 51
e-mail: maeusezahl@ubachs.unibas.ch

McEowen Carol (USA)
Habitat Group, Architekturabteilung
ETH Zürich-Hönggerberg
CH-8093 Zürich Switzerland
Tel. +41 1 633 28 17
Fax: +41 1 633 10 63

Mechkat Cyrus
Institut Universitaire d'Etudes du
Développement (IUED)
24, rue Rothschild, C.P. 136
CH-1211 Genève 21 Switzerland
Tel. +41 22 906 59 64
Fax: +41 22 906 59 47
e-mail: mechkat@uni2.unige.ch

Mejia Mejia Margarita (Portugal)
Center for African Studies
University Eduardo Mondlane
C.P. 1993
Maputo Mozambique
Tel. +258 1 49 08 28
Fax: +258 1 49 18 96

Menzi Martin
Mittlere Ringstrasse 5
CH-3600 Thun Switzerland
Tel. +41 33 22 85 32
Fax: +41 33 22 85 76

Messerli Bruno
Institute of Geography
University of Berne
Hallerstrasse 12
CH-3012 Bern Switzerland
Tel. +41 31 631 80 18
Fax: +41 31 631 85 11
e-mail: messerli@giub.unibe.ch

Meyer Thomas
Hauptstrasse 26
CH-4105 Biel-Benken Switzerland
Tel. +41 61 721 18 66

Milbert Isabelle (France)
Institut Universitaire d'Etudes
du Développement (IUED)
24, rue Rothschild, C.P. 136
CH-1211 Genève 21 Switzerland
Tel. +41 22 906 59 40
Fax: +41 22 906 59 47
e-mail: milbert@uni2a.unige.ch

Mokhele Khotso
Foundation for Research Development (FRD)
P.O. Box 2600
0001 Pretoria South Africa
Tel. +27 12 481 40 83
Fax: +27 12 481 40 06
e-mail: pulane@frd.ac.za

Moll Martin
GEONEX
Rütistrasse 20
CH-8952 Schlieren Switzerland
Tel. & Fax: +41 1 730 74 64
e-mail: geonex@spectraweb.ch

Monnier Laurent
Institut Universitaire d'Etudes
du Développement (IUED)
24, rue Rothschild, C.P. 136
CH-1211 Genève 21 Switzerland
Tel. +41 22 906 59 63 / Fax: ... 47

Moreno Juan Carlos (Spain)
Radio Suisse International
Giacommettistrasse 1
CH-3015 Bern Switzerland
Tel. +41 31 350 92 22 / Fax: ... 95 69

Mühlebach Andrea
Erlensträsschen 62
CH-4125 Riehen Switzerland
Tel. +41 61 641 08 38

Mühlemann Marc
Institute of Biochemistry
University of Berne
Freiestrasse 3
CH-3012 Bern Switzerland
Tel. +41 31 631 43 40
Fax: +41 31 631 48 87
e-mail: huebner@ibc.unibe.ch

Musy André
Institut d'aménagement des terres
et des eaux (IATE)
EPF Lausanne
CH-1015 Lausanne Switzerland
Tel. +41 21 693 37 25
Fax: +41 21 693 37 39
e-mail: musu@dgn.epfl.ch.

Mwenesi Halima (Kenya)
Swiss Tropical Institute (STI)
Socinstrasse 57, P.O. Box
CH-4002 Basel Switzerland
Tel. +41 61 284 82 21
Fax: +41 61 271 79 51

Mwenya Wilson N.M.
Ministry of Science, Technology and
Vocational Training, P.O. Box 50464
Lusaka Zambia
Tel. +260 1 25 19 53
Fax: +260 1 25 29 51

Naciri Mohammed
Institut Agronomique et Vétérinaire
Université Hassan II
5, rue Jaber Ibn Hayane
Rabat Morocco
Tel. +212 7 77 03 55

Nair K.N.
Centre for Development Studies (CDS)
Prasanthnagar Road, Ulloor
Thiruvananthapuram
695011 Kerala India
Tel. +91 471 44 88 81
Fax: +91 471 44 71 37

Najafbagy Reza
Comparative Management &
Organization Theories
Azad University, P.O. Box 19395
5153 Tehran Iran
Tel. +9821 225 06 05
Fax: +98 21 225 32 58

Ndao Momar
Institut de Médecine Tropicale
Nationalestraat 155
B-2000 Antwerpen Belgium
Tel. +32 3 247 63 68
Fax: +32 3 247 63 73
e-mail: Pdorny@itg.be

Ndegwa Elijah N.D.
DURP
University of Nairobi
P.O. Box 30197
Nairobi Kenya
Tel. +254 234 09 72
Fax: +254 271 85 48

N'Dhiekor Yemadji
Swiss Tropical Institute (STI)
B.P. 972
N'Djamena Chad
Tel. +235 52 30 60
Fax: +235 52 26 63

Ndione Emmanuel Seyni
Environment and Development
for Africa (ENDA / GRAF)
P.O. Box 13069
Dakar Senegal
Tel. +221 27 20 25
Fax: +221 27 32 15

Nebiker Hans-Rudolf
National Concillor
Hofgut Ebnet
CH-4457 Diegten Switzerland
Tel. +41 61 971 15 11
Fax: +41 61 971 19 40

Part IV — List and Addresses of Participants

Neuhaus Gabriela
SF DRS Redaktion MTW
Fernsehstrasse 1-4, P.O. Box
CH-8052 Zürich Switzerland
Tel. +41 1 305 58 97 / Fax: ... 80

Neversil Barbara
Schweizerische Depeschenagentur (AG/SDA)
Länggassstrasse 7
Postfach
CH-3001 Bern Switzerland
Tel. +41 31 309 33 33
Fax: +41 31 301 85 38

Ngugi George
DURP
University of Nairobi
P.O. Box 30197
Nairobi Kenya
Tel. +254 234 09 72
Fax: +254 271 85 48

Niangado Oumar
Institut d'économie rurale (IER)
Avenue Mohamed V, C.P. 258
Bamako Mali
Tel. +223 22 55 73
Fax: +223 22 37 75
e-mail: niangado@ver-dir.ver.ml

Nicolier Felix Ludwig
Ciba-Geigy Foundation for Cooperation with Developing Countries
Klybeckstrasse 141, P.O. Box
CH-4002 Basel Switzerland
Tel. +41 61 696 13 17
Fax: +41 61 696 22 39

Nienstedt Karin Monica
Institute of Plantpathology & Plantprotection
University of Hannover
Herrenhäuserstrasse 2
D-30419 Hannover Germany
Tel. +49 511 762 35 02
Fax: +49 511 762 30 15
e-mail: nienstedt@mbox.ipp.uni-hannover.de

Njagi Seraphin B.
DURP
University of Nairobi
P.O. Box 30197
Nairobi Kenya
Tel. +254 234 09 72
Fax: +254 271 85 48

Nkwi Paul Nchoji
International Centre for Applied Social Science
P.O. Box 1862
Yaounde Cameroun
Tel. +237 23 42 27
Fax: +237 22 18 73
e-mail: icassrt@cam.healthnet.org

North Nicole
INFRAS, Rieterstrasse 18
CH-8002 Zürich Switzerland
Tel. +41 1 202 93 14
Fax: +41 1 202 33 65

Nowak Stefan
Polygon
University of Fribourg, Pérolles
CH-1700 Fribourg Switzerland
Tel. +41 37 29 73 30
Fax: +41 37 29 97 28
e-mail: stefan.nowak@unifr.ch

Nuyens Yvo (Belgium)
Council on Health Research for Development (COHRED)
Palais des Nations
CH-1211 Genève 10 Switzerland
Tel. +41 22 979 95 58
Fax: +41 22 979 90 15

Oberti Jean
CIHEAM-IAMM
3191, route de Mende, C.P. 5056
F-34033 Montpellier Cedex 1 France
Tel. +33 67 04 60 63
Fax: +33 67 54 25 27
e-mail: oberti@iamm.fr

Odermatt Peter
Swiss Tropical Institute (STI)
Socinstrasse 57, P.O. Box
CH-4002 Basel Switzerland
Tel. +41 61 284 82 83
Fax: +41 61 271 79 51
e-mail: odermatt@ubaclu.unibas.ch

Oetliker Sybille
Redaktion "Cash", P.O. Box
CH-3000 Bern 7 Switzerland
Tel. +41 31 311 45 38
Fax: +41 31 312 38 40

Okafor Nduka
Foundation for African Develop. through International Biotechnology (FADIB)

P.O. Box 1457
Enugu Nigeria
Tel. +234 42 45 93 60
Fax: +234 42 45 32 02
e-mail: fadib@rcl.dircon.co.uk

Onken Thomas
National Councillor
Lehrinstitut Onken AG
CH-8280 Kreuzlingen Switzerland
Tel. +41 71 672 44 44
Fax: +41 71 672 55 62

Ortega Liliane
Swiss Agency for Development and
Cooperation (SDC)
Section West-Africa
Eigerstrasse 80
CH-3003 Bern
Tel. +41 31 322 34 62
Fax: +41 31 324 16 95
e-mail: liliane.ortega@sdc.admin.ch

Ott Cordula
Group for Development &
Environment (GfEU)
Institute of Geography
University of Berne
CH-3012 Bern Switzerland
Tel. +41 31 631 88 22
Fax: +41 31 631 85 44

Ottiger Nadja
ETH Zürich Zentrum
Rämistrasse 101
CH-8092 Zürich Switzerland
Tel. +41 1 632 32 24
Fax: +41 1 632 11 10

Ouayogodé Bakary
Department of Education and
Scientific Research
Tour E 20è, C.P. V 151
Abidjan Ivory Cost
Tel. +225 21 36 20
Fax: +225 21 22 25

Ousseini Issa
Département de géographie
Université A.M. Niamey
C.P. 418
Niamey Niger
Tel. +227 74 00 68
Fax: +227 72 30 36

Owais Wajih M.
Faculty of Science
Yarmouk University
Irbid Jordan
Tel. +962 2 7 11 00
Fax: +962 2 24 79 83

Packer Ignacio John
European Association for Development
and Health (AEDES)
34, rue Joseph II
B-1040 Brussels Belgium
Tel. +32 2 219 03 06
Fax: +32 2 219 09 38

Péguy Alain (France)
Ambassade de France
Schosshaldenstrasse 46, P.O. Box
CH-3000 Bern 32 Switzerland
Tel. +41 31 359 21 36
Fax: +41 31 359 21 92

Petschek Peter
Ingenieurschule Interkantonales
Technikum Rapperswil (ITR)
Oberseestrasse 10
CH-8640 Rapperswil Switzerland
Tel. +41 55 23 41 11
Fax: +41 55 23 44 00
e-mail: petschek@itr.ch.

Pfister Jürg
Schweizerischer Nationalfonds (SNF)
Wildhainweg 20
CH-3001 Bern Switzerland
Tel. +41 31 308 22 34
Fax: +41 31 301 30 09
e-mail: chb59jpf@ibmmail.com

Plancherel Jean-Marie
CFRC Coopération
EPF Lausanne
CH-1015 Lausanne Switzerland
Tel. +41 21 693 30 12
Fax: +41 21 693 60 10

Poddar Prakash
West Bengal Voluntary Health Association
19A, Dr. Sundari Nlohan Avenue
700014 Calcutta India
Tel. +91 33 244 67 54
Fax: +91 33 248 16 20

Poltera Anton Alexander
Schweizerisches Serum- und Impfinstitut
Rehagstrasse 79, P.O. Box

CH-3018 Bern Switzerland
Tel. +41 31 980 61 11
Fax: +41 31 980 67 75

Poretti Fabrizio
Gewerbestrasse 22
CH-3012 Bern Switzerland
Tel. +41 31 302 85 49

Poswal M. Ashraf
International Institute of Biological Control
P.O. Box 8
Rawalpindi Pakistan
Tel. +92 51 42 32 10
Fax: +92 51 45 11 47

Preti Véronique
Schweizerischer Nationalfonds (SNF)
Wildhainweg 20
CH-3001 Bern Switzerland
Tel. +41 31 308 22 22
Fax: +41 31 301 30 09

Priestley Carol
International Africa Institute (IAI)
Thornhaugh Street, Russel Square
London WC 1H OXG United Kingdom
Tel. +44 171 323 6035
Fax: +44 171 323 6118
e-mail: cpriestley@gn.apc.org

Probala Rolf
SF DRS "Tagesschau"
P.O. Box
CH-8052 Zürich Switzerland
Tel. +41 1 305 66 11
Fax: +41 1 305 56 60

Purser Lewis (Ireland)
Institut Universitaire d'Etudes
du Développement (IUED)
24, rue Rothschild, C.P. 136
CH-1211 Genève 21 Switzerland
Tel. +41 22 906 59 40
Fax: +41 22 906 59 47

Quansah Nathaniel
WWF Ethnobotany Project
WWF Country Office
P.O. Box 738
Antananarivo 101 Madagascar
Tel. +261 2 348 85
Fax: +261 2 348 88
e-mail: aires.pr@wwf.wwf.mg

Raguram Ramanathan
Nimhans
560 029 Bangalore India
Tel. +91 80 64 91 54
Fax: +91 845 21 86 NIMH IN
e-mail: nnic@ren.nic.in

Rapp Jean-Philippe
Télévision Suisse Romande (TSI)
C.P. 234
CH-1211 Genève 8 Switzerland
Tel. +41 22 708 99 11
Fax: +41 22 708 98 29

Reichmuth Markus
FUNDES
Hauptstrasse 10, P.O. Box
CH-8872 Weesen Switzerland
Tel. +41 58 43 66 62
Fax: +41 58 43 66 51

Reigota Marcos
Rua Nhambiquaras 11
17.600 Tupa
Sao Paulo Brazil
Tel. +55 144 42 53 35
Fax: +55 11 577 51 83

Rieder Peter
Swiss Center for International
Agriculture (ZIL)
ETH Zürich
Sonneggstrasse 33
CH-8092 Zürich Switzerland
Tel. +41 1 632 53 07
Fax: +41 1 632 10 86
e-mail: rieder@iaw.agrl.ethz.ch

Riond Jean-Luc
Institut für Veterinär-Physiologie
University of Zürich
Winterthurerstrasse 260
CH-8057 Zürich Switzerland
Tel. +41 1 365 14 67
Fax: +41 1 365 13 23
e-mail: jriond@vetphys.unizh.ch

Romero Hugo
Escuela de Post-Grado
Facultad de Arquitectura y Urbanismo
University of Chile
Marcoleta 250, P.O. Box 3387
Santiago de Chile Chile
Tel. +56 2 678 31 12
Fax: +56 2 222 95 22
e-mail: hromero@abello.dic.uchile.cl

Part IV   List and Addresses of Participants

Royer Jacques
Centre universitaire d'étude des problèmes
de l'énergie (CUEPE)
Université de Genève
4, chemin de Conches
CH-1231 Conches Switzerland
Tel. +41 22 789 13 11
Fax: +41 22 347 86 49
e-mail: jacques.royer@cuepe.unige.ch

Rübel Alex
Zoo Zürich
Zürichbergstrasse 221
CH-8044 Zürich Switzerland
Tel. +41 1 251 54 11
Fax: +41 1 261 31 24
e-mail: zoozh@dial.eunet.ch

Rüdinger Erik
Ministry of Foreign Affairs
Department for Evaluation, Research
and Documentation
2, Asiatisk Plads
DK-1448 Copenhagen Denmark
Tel. +45 33 92 09 44 / Fax: ... 04 93

Rüegg Jacob
Swiss Federal Research Station
CH-8820 Wädenswil Switzerland
Tel. +41 1 783 64 28
Fax: +41 1 780 63 41

Ruiz-Rios Luis Miguel
International Organization for Migration
(IOM)
Division of Migration for Development
17, route des Morillons
CH-1211 Genève 19 Switzerland
Tel. +41 22 717 93 62
Fax: +41 22 798 61 50
e-mail: ruiz@geneva.iom.ch

Rwezaura Juliet
P.O. Box 1959
Dar-es-Salaam Tanzania
Tel. +255 51 278 60
Fax: +255 51 460 69

Sabelli Fabrizio (Italy)
Institut Universitaire d'Etudes
du Développement (IUED)
24, rue Rothschild, C.P. 136
CH-1211 Genève 21 Switzerland
Tel. +41 22 906 59 92
Fax: +41 22 906 59 47

Salem-Kalali Hossein (Iran)
10, Boulevard de la Tour
CH-1205 Genève Switzerland
Tel. +41 22 328 00 66
Fax: +41 22 735 58 10

Sami Kriaa (Tunesia)
Ingénieurs du Monde EPFL
Centre-midi EPF Lausanne
CH-1015 Ecublens Switzerland
Tel. +41 21 693 20 45

Sandala Landasa (Zaire)
17, Fin de la Croix
CH-1762 Givisiez Switzerland
Tel. +41 37 26 88 21
e-mail: landasa.sandala@unifr.ch

Sanglier Perine
AIRE développement
45bis, avenue de la Belle Gabrielle
F-94736 Nogent-sur-Marne France
Tel. +33 1 43 94 44 15 / Fax: ... 39
e-mail: tricornot@aire.orstom.fr

Sanoja Elio
Laboratorio de Botanica
Universidad Nacional Experimental
de Guyana (UNEG)
Ave. Valmora Rodriguez
Upata - Estado Bolivar Venezuela
Tel. & Fax: +58 88 212 193
e-mail: esanoja@dino.conicit.ve

Sansonnens Bertrand
Institut de botanique (IBSG)
Université de Lausanne
CH-1015 Lausanne Switzerland
Tel. +41 21 692 42 60 / Fax: ... 65

Sarnaik Jayant
Applied Environmental Research Foundation
Ganga-Tara Apt. 917/7
Ganesh Wadi
411 004 Pune India
Tel. +91 212 350 239
Fax: +91 212 639 203

Sauvain-Dugeroil Claudine
Laboratoire de démographie
Université de Genève
2, rue Dancet
CH-1211 Genève 4 Switzerland
Tel. +41 22 705 71 08
Fax: +41 22 320 91 25
e-mail: sauvain@ibm.unige.ch

Part IV List and Addresses of Participants

Savary Claude
Musée d'ethnographie
C.P. 191
CH-1211 Genève 8 Switzerland
Tel. +41 22 418 45 49
Fax: +41 22 328 52 31

Schaer Jean Paul
Institut de géologie
11, rue Emile-Argand
CH-2007 Neuchâtel Switzerland
Tel. +41 38 23 26 63
Fax: +41 38 23 26 01
e-mail: schaer@geol.unine.ch

Schäublin Christoph H.
Rectorate of the University of Berne
Hochschulstrasse 4
CH-3012 Bern Switzerland
Tel. +41 31 631 80 07
Fax: +41 31 631 39 39

Scheidegger Urs
Schweizerische Ingenieurschule
für Landwirtschaft (SIL)
Länggasse 85
CH-3052 Zollikofen Switzerland
Tel. +41 31 910 21 71
Fax: +41 31 910 22 96

Schertenleib Roland
Swiss Federal Institute for Environment,
Science and Technology (EAWAG)
Überlandstrasse 133
CH-8600 Dübendorf Switzerland
Tel. +41 1 823 50 18
Fax: +41 1 823 53 99
e-mail: schertenleib@eawag.ch

Schmid Willy A.
ORL-Institut
ETH Zürich Hönggerberg
CH-8093 Zürich Switzerland
Tel. +41 1 633 29 57
Fax: +41 1 633 11 02
e-mail: schmid@orl.arch.ethz.ch

Schneider Fritz
Schweizerische Ingenieurschule für
Landwirtschaft (SIL)
Länggasse 85
CH-3052 Zollikofen Switzerland
Tel. +41 31 910 21 71
Fax: +41 31 910 22 96

Schneider Jürg
Institute of Ethnology
University of Berne
Länggassstrasse 49a
CH-3003 Bern Switzerland
Tel. +41 31 631 89 99 / Fax: ... 42 12
e-mail: schneider@ethno.unibe.ch

Schöpf Karl
Bundesanstalt für Veterinärmedizin
Langer Weg 27
A-6020 Innsbruck Austria
Tel. +43 512 34 87 90
Fax: +43 512 39 45 18

Schwank Othmar
INFRAS
Rieterstrasse 18
CH-8002 Zürich Switzerland
Tel. +41 1 202 93 14
Fax: +41 1 202 33 65

Sharan Hari (Indian)
Dasag Energy Engineering Ltd.
Birchstrasse 6
CH-8472 Seuzach Switzerland
Tel. +41 52 335 35 00 / Fax: ... 14 42
e-mail: 100343.210@compuserve.com

Shumbusho Lambert
Université de Neuchâtel
2, avenue du 1er Mars
CH-2000 Neuchâtel Switzerland
Tel. +41 38 24 36 36 / Fax: ... 55 79

Siegmund Thomas
Institute for Microenterprise
Development in Latin America
Margarethenweg 11
A-4020 Linz Austria
Tel. +43 732 77 08 58
Fax: +43 732 78 24 75

Simmen Rosmarie
National Councillor
Rosenweg 23
CH-4500 Solothurn Switzerland
Tel. +41 65 22 95 52
Fax: +41 65 23 67 87

Sindayigaya Oscar (Burundi)
EPF Lausanne
Bât. LESO
CH-1015 Lausanne Switzerland
Tel. +41 21 693 45 45
Fax: +41 21 693 27 22

Part IV — List and Addresses of Participants

Singh Véronique
Journal de Genève
12, rue de Itesse
CH-1211 Genève Switzerland
Tel. & Fax: +41 66 22 48 45

Sitter-Liver Beat
Swiss Academy of Humanities and
Social Sciences
Hirschengraben 11, P.O. Box 8160
CH-3001 Bern Switzerland
Tel. +41 31 311 33 76 / Fax: ... 91 64

Smits Paul
Advisory Council for Scientific Research
in Development Problems (RAWOO)
P.O. Box 29777
NL-2502 LT The Hague The Netherlands
Tel. +31 70 426 03 31
Fax: +31 70 426 03 29

Smyke Raymond J.
5, chemin du Banc-Vert
CH-1110 Morges Switzerland
Tel. +41 21 801 69 83 / Fax: ... 99 01

Som Claudia
EMPA St. Gallen
Abteilung Ökologie und Kreislauf
Unterstrasse 11
CH-9001 St.Gallen Switzerland
Tel. +41 71 30 01 01
Fax: +41 71 30 01 99
e-mail: claudia.som@empa.ch

Sottas Beat
Verwaltungskontrolle des Bundesrates
Marktgasse 52
CH-3003 Bern Switzerland
Tel. +41 31 322 70 46
Fax: +41 31 322 70 01
e-mail: beat.sottas@bk.admin.ch

Spack Simone
Blumenrain 28
CH-2503 Biel Switzerland
Tel. +41 32 25 66 02

Spillmann Kurt R.
Forschungsstelle für Sicherheits-
politik und Konfliktanalyse
ETH Zentrum
CH-8092 Zürich Switzerland
Tel. +41 1 632 40 25
Fax: +41 1 363 91 96
e-mail: spillmann@sipo.reok.ethz.ch

Srivastava Leena
TATA Energy Research Institute
Darbari Seth Block, Habitat Center
Lodi Road
110 003 New Delhi India
Tel. +91 11 462 22 46
Fax: +91 11 462 17 70
e-mail: leena@teri.ernet.in

Stähelin Fritz Rudolf
Swiss Peace Foundation
Weiermattring 38
CH-5200 Brugg Switzerland
Tel. & Fax: +41 56 441 84 37

Staubli Franziska
Institute for Food Science
Laboratory for Human Nutrition
ETH Zürich
Seestrasse 72, P.O. Box 474
CH-8803 Rüschlikon Switzerland
Tel. +41 1 724 27 77
Fax: +41 1 724 01 83

Stearns Steven (USA)
Institute of Zoology
University of Basle
Rheinsprung 9
CH-4051 Basel Switzerland
Tel. +41 61 267 34 85
Fax: +41 61 267 34 57
e-mail: stearns@ubaclu.unibas.ch

Stenersen Christian
Les Rossanets-Segny
F-01170 Gex France
Tel. +33 50 41 78 80

Stich August H.R.
Medical Mission Institute
Salvatorstrasse 7
D-97074 Würzburg Germany
Tel. +49 931 791 29 00
Fax: +49 931 791 28 01

Strombom Bo (Sweden)
International Management
Services (IMS)
36, chemin de la Forêt
CH-1009 Pully Switzerland
Tel. +41 22 950 04 24
Fax: +41 22 950 04 21
e-mail: bostrom@iprolink.ch

Part IV List and Addresses of Participants

Stückelberger Christoph
Bread for all
Speichergasse 29, P.O. Box
CH-3000 Bern 7 Switzerland
Tel. +41 31 312 32 35
Fax: +41 31 311 54 91
e-mail: bfa@bfd.link-ch1.ch

Stump Therese
Swiss Agency for Development
and Cooperation (SDC)
Eigerstrasse 73
CH-3007 Bern Switzerland
Tel. +41 31 322 34 75
Fax: +41 31 324 16 91

Taboada Wilma Varinia (Argentina)
RATP
2, av. de la Constellation
F-95800 Cergy France
Tel. +33 30 32 36 08
Fax: +33 44 68 23 10

Tâche Christian
EICN / LEMI
7, Hôtel de Ville
CH-2400 Le Locle Switzerland
Tel. +41 39 34 12 12
Fax: +41 39 31 26 07
e-mail: tache@eicn.etna.ch

Tanner Marcel
Swiss Tropical Institute (STI)
Socinstrasse 57, P.O. Box
CH-4002 Basel Switzerland
Tel. +41 61 284 82 83
Fax: +41 61 271 79 51
e-mail: tanner@ubaclu.unibas.ch

Thierstein Hans Rudolf
Institute of Geology
ETH Zürich Zentrum
Sonneggstrasse 5
CH-8092 Zürich Switzerland
Tel. +41 1 632 36 66
Fax: +41 1 632 10 51
e-mail: thierstein@erdw.ethz.ch

Thulstrup Erik W.
Institute of Life Sciences & Chemistry
Roskilde University
P.O. Box 260
DK-4000 Roskilde Denmark
Tel. +45 46 75 77 11
Fax: +45 46 75 77 21
e-mail: ewt@mmf.ruc.dk

Tobler-Rohr Marion Irène
Group for Environmental Hygiene
ETH Zürich
CH-8093 Zürich Switzerland
Tel. +41 1 633 33 07
Fax: +41 1 633 10 69

Trevelyan Rosie
Tropical Biology Association (TBA)
University of Bristol
Woodland Road
Bristol Avon BS8 1 UG United Kingdom
Tel. & Fax: +44 117 929 33 38
e-mail: bristol-tba@bris.ac.uk

Trutmann Peter
Swiss Centre for International
Agriculture (ZIL)
ETH Zürich
Sonneneggstrasse 53
CH-8092 Zürich Switzerland
Tel. +41 1 632 53 31
Fax: +41 1 632 10 86
e-mail: trutmann@iaw.agrl.ethz.ch

Ubi Anthony (Niger)
Institute of Food Science
and Technology (LFO)
ETH Zürich
CH-8092 Zürich Switzerland
Tel. +41 1 632 36 61
Fax: +41 1 632 11 23

Uplekar Mukund
Community Health
84-A RG Thadani Marg, Worli
400018 Bombay India
Tel. +91 22 493 86 01
Fax: +91 22 493 31 87
e-mail: narayan@shakti.ncst.ernet.in

Utting Peter (Australia)
United Nations Research Institute
for Social Development (UNRISD)
Palais des Nations
CH-1211 Genève Switzerland
Tel. +41 22 798 84 00
Fax: +41 22 740 07 91

Utzinger Jürg
Swiss Tropical Institute (STI)
Socinstrasse 57, P.O. Box
CH-4002 Basel Switzerland
Tel. +41 61 284 82 83
Fax: +41 61 271 79 51
e-mail: odermatt@ubaclu.unibas.ch

Van Eer Aissah (The Netherlands)
Seevilla
Esplanade 20, Top 2
A-4810 Gmunden Austria
Tel. +43 761 27 77 83

Van Westrienen Gerard
Advisory Council RAWOO
P.O. Box 29777
NL-2502 The Hague The Netherlands
Tel. +31 70 426 03 31 / Fax: ... 29

Vauthey Barbara
Euro-Guichet
Université de Fribourg, Pérolles
CH-1700 Fribourg Switzerland
Tel. +41 37 29 73 32
Fax: +41 37 29 97 28
e-mail: barbara.vauthey@unifr.ch

Véron René
Institute of Geography
University of Zurich
Winterthurerstrasse 190
CH-8057 Zürich Switzerland
Tel. +41 1 257 51 87
Fax: +41 1 362 52 27
e-mail: rveron@gis.geogr.unizh.ch

Von Graffenried Charlotte
Brunnadernrain 3B
CH-3006 Bern Switzerland
Tel. & Fax: +41 31 352 70 22

Vu Duc Trinh (Vietnam)
Institut de Santé au Travail (IST)
19, rue du Bugnon
CH-1005 Lausanne Switzerland
Tel. +41 21 314 74 21 / Fax: ... 20
e-mail: trinh.vuduc@inst.hospvd.ch

Waas Eveline
Alter Ego / Urbaplan
21, avenue Montchoisi, C.P. 151
CH-1000 Lausanne 19 Switzerland
Tel. +41 21 616 66 66 / Fax: ... 41 31

Waast Roland
Institut français de recherche scientifique
pour le développement en coopération
(ORSTOM)
72, route d'Aulnay
F-93143 Bondy Cedex France
Tel. +33 1 48 02 55 00
Fax: +33 1 48 47 30 88
e-mail: waast@bondy.orstom.fr

Wacker Corinne
Department of Social Anthropology
University of Zürich
Mühlegasse 21
CH-8001 Zürich Switzerland
Tel. +41 1 257 68 32
Fax: +41 1 257 69 97
e-mail: wacker@ethno.uniz.ch

Waldner Rosmarie D.
Redaktion Tages-Anzeiger
P.O. Box
CH-8021 Zürich Switzerland
Tel. +41 1 248 44 11
Fax: +41 1 248 44 71

Waldvogel Francis
Council of the Swiss Federal Institutes of Technology
ETH Zentrum HAB
CH-8092 Zürich Switzerland
Tel. +41 1 632 20 02
Fax: +41 1 632 11 90

Walter Paul
Biochemisches Institut im Vesalianum
University of Basle
Vesalgasse 1
CH-4051 Basel Switzerland
Tel. +41 61 267 35 61
Fax: +41 61 267 35 66

Wälty Samuel
Institute of Geography
University of Zürich
Winterthurerstrasse 190
CH-8057 Zürich Switzerland
Tel. +41 1 257 51 87
Fax: +41 1 362 52 27
e-mail: waelty@gis.geogr.unizh.ch

Wehrli Christoph
Neue Zürcher Zeitung (NZZ)
P.O. Box
CH-8021 Zürich Switzerland
Tel. +41 1 258 10 27
Fax: +41 1 252 13 29

Weidmann Brigitte
Infoagrar
c/o Schweizerische Ingenieurschule
für Landwirtschaft (SIL)
Länggasse 85
CH-3052 Zollikofen Switzerland
Tel. +41 31 910 21 91
Fax: +41 31 910 21 54

Part IV List and Addresses of Participants

Weiss Mitchell (USA)
Swiss Tropical Institute (STI)
Socinstrasse 57, P.O. Box
CH-4002 Basel Switzerland
Tel. +41 61 284 82 90
Fax: +41 61 271 79 51
e-mail: weissm@ubaclu.unibas.ch

Wesley-Tanaskovic Ines
United Nations University Tokyo Japan
c/o ICTP
P.O. Box 586
I-34100 Trieste Italy
Tel. +39 40 22 499 11
Fax: +39 40 22 46 00
e-mail: wesley@ictp.trieste.it

Wespi Yvonne
Ingénieurs du Monde
EPF Lausanne
CH-1015 Lausanne Switzerland
Tel. +41 21 693 20 45
Fax: +41 21 693 60 10
e-mail: yvonne.wespi@ibois.dgc.epfl.ch

Wiesmann Urs
Group for Development and
Environment (GfEU)
Institute of Geography
University of Berne
Hallerstrasse 12
CH-3012 Bern Switzerland
Tel. +41 31 631 88 75
Fax: +41 31 631 85 44
e-mail: wiesmann@giub.unibe.ch

Wilhelm Rolf
Haltenstrasse 251
CH-3145 Oberscherli Switzerland
Tel. +41 31 849 10 18
Fax: +41 31 849 21 35

Williams Robert J.
CAB International
Wallingford
Oxon OX10 8DE United Kingdom
Tel. +44 1491 832 111
Fax: +44 1491 833 508
e-mail: r.williams@cabi.org

Winistörfer Jörg
Institut de Géographie
Université de Lausanne
CH-1015 Lausanne Switzerland
Tel. +41 21 692 30 72
Fax: +41 21 692 44 98

Wohlhauser Sébastien
Laboratoire de phanérogamie botanique
Université de Neuchâtel
Chantemerle 22
CH-2007 Neuchâtel Switzerland
Tel. +41 38 23 23 47
Fax: +41 38 23 30 01

Wolf Markus
Institute of Plantbiology
University of Zürich
Zollikerstrasse 107
CH-8008 Zürich Switzerland
Tel. +41 1 385 42 38
Fax: +41 1 385 42 04

Wurapa Frederick K.
WHO Regional Office for Africa
P.O. Box 6
Brazzaville Congo
Tel. +242 83 91 11
Fax: +242 83 94 00
e-mail: afro@who.org

Wyss Kaspar
Swiss Tropical Institute (STI)
Socinstrasse 57, P.O. Box
CH-4002 Basel Switzerland
Tel. +41 61 284 82 29
Fax: +41 61 271 79 51
e-mail: odermatt@ubaclu.unibas.ch

Yang Charles
Asian Vegetable Research and Development
Center (AVRDC), Asian Regional Center
P.O. Box 9-1010
10903 Bangkok Thailand
Tel. +66 2 579 55 35
Fax: +66 2 561 48 88

Zapotoczky Klaus
Österreichische Forschungsstiftung
für Entwicklungshilfe (ÖFSE)
Berggasse 7
A-1090 Wien Austria
Tel. +43 1 317 40 10
Fax: +43 1 317 40 15

Zhuwau Tom
Blair Research Laboratories
Ministry of Health Zimbabwe
Causeway
Harare Zimbabwe
Tel. +263 4 792 747

Zinsmeister Cornelia
Am Sunnaberg 11
FL-9495 Triesen Liechtenstein
Tel. & Fax: +41 75 392 17 71
e-mail: 101673.567@compuserve.com

Zolezzi Lorenzo
Facultad de Derecho
Universidad Pontificia Catolica del Peru
Lima Peru
Tel. +51 14 623 501
Fax: +51 14 611 785
e-mail: lzolezz@pucp.edu.pe

Zubler Kurt
Pestalozzistrasse 40
CH-8200 Schaffhausen Switzerland

Zumbühl Monika
Swiss Institute of Development (SID)
Bözingenstrasse 71
CH-2502 Biel Switzerland
Tel. +41 32 52 30 50
Fax: +41 32 41 08 10
e-mail: sid@dial.eunet.ch

Zürcher Markus
Swiss Academy of Humanities and
Social Sciences
Hirschengraben 11, P.O. Box 8160
CH-3001 Bern Switzerland
Tel. +41 31 311 33 76
Fax: +41 31 311 91 64

Zwahlen François
Centre d'hydrogéologie (CHYNE)
Université de Neuchâtel
11, rue Emile-Argand
CH-2007 Neuchâtel Switzerland
Tel. +41 38 23 26 89
Fax: +41 38 23 26 01
e-mail: françois.zwahlen@chyne.unine.ch

Zweifel Helen
Group for Development and
Environment (GfEU)
Institute of Geography
University of Berne
Hallerstrasse 12
CH-3012 Bern Switzerland
Tel. +41 31 631 37 52
Fax: +41 31 631 85 44
e-mail: zweifel@giub.unibe.ch

compiled by Cornelia Zinsmeister & Daniel Maselli

Part IV   Annex

Poster Exhibition: List of Themes and Contact Persons

The following list contains - in alphabetical order of the titles - all the posters presented at the Conference with the names of the institutions and people involved. Addresses of contact-persons can be found in the "List and Addresses of Participants" (Part IV).

"Academic Partnership and University Teaching in African History"
Basel Mission Archive; Basle, Presbyterian Church in Cameroon; Protestant Chaplaincy, Univ. of Heidelberg; IG Afrikanische Geschichte, Basle; *P. Jenkins, Jonas Dah*

"Actors' Strategies and Perceptions (ASP) for Sustainable Resource Management and Planning"
Univ. of Berne& Univ. of Nairobi; *B. Sottas, U. Wiesmann, M. Flury, G. King'oriah G. Ngugi, E.N.D. Ndegwa, C. Eggmann Betschart, E. Künzi, F. Maina, S. Njagi*

"Anomie Research: Preventing Breakdown of Societies"
Swiss Inst. for Development (SID), Biel; *P. Atteslander*

"Antibacterial Potency of Medical Plants Used in Traditional Medicine in Côte d'Ivoire"
Centre Suisse de Recherche Scientifique Côte d'Ivoire (CSRS); Laboratoire de botanique végétale, Univ. d'Abidjan, Côte d'Ivoire & Inst. of Pharmacy, Basle; *C.R. Weiss, Kamanzi K. Atindenou, H.G. Téré, W. Schaffner*

"Application of Molecluar Genetics for the Management of Aromatics in Waste"
National Environmental Engineering Research Inst. (NEERI), Nagpur; Inst. of Biotechnology, ETH Zurich; Swiss Federal Inst. of Environmental Science and Technology (EAWAG), Dübendorf; *H. Purohit, P. Khanna, K. Jenny, J.-R. van der Meer*

"Bioprocess Development and Genetic Manipulation in Microbial Systems"
Maharaja Sayajirao Univ., Baroda, Indo-Swiss Collaboration in Biotechnology, Inst. of Biotech. ETHZ, Zurich; *B. B. Chattoo, K. Jenny, Armin Fiechter, Jay Baily, Bernard Witholt*

"Bioprocess Development with Biological Pesticides Active against Mosquitoes and Agricultural Insect Pests"
Anna Univ., Madras, Inst. of Biotechnology, ETH Zurich, Inst. de Genie Chimique, EPF Lausanne; *K. Jayaraman, K. Jenny, Armin Fiechter, Ian Marison, Urs von Stockar*

"Biosafety Research and Assessment of Technology Impacts of Swiss Priority Programme Biotechnology (BATS)"
BATS, Basle; *O. Käppeli, Elisabeth Schulte*

"Biotechnology in Africa: An Ideal Meeting-Point for North-South Collaboration"
Foundation for African Dev. through International Biotechnology (FADIB); *E. N. Okafor*

"Capitalisation of Community Based Initiatives in the Urban Environment of N'Djamena (Chad)"
Bureau appui santé et environment (BASE), N'Djamena & Swiss Tropical Inst. (STI), Basle; *Y. N'Dhiekhor, K. Wyss, Emile Jeannée*

"Collaborative Research Program on Sleeping Sickness in Uganda"
Swiss Tropical Inst. (STI), Basel, Livestock Health Research Inst., Tororo; *R. Brun, R. Kaminsky, J. Enyaru*

Part IV   Poster Exhibition: List of Themes and Contact Persons

"Cooperation Mali - Switzerland: Forestry Research Program of Sikasso"
Intercoopération (IC), Berne & Inst. d'économie rurale (IER), Bamako; *Pascal Cuny, Nicolas Bagnoud, M. Chollet*

"Cycle postgrade sur le développement"
Swiss Federal Inst. of Technology, Lausanne (EPFL) & Ecole inter-états d'ingénieurs de l'équipement rural (EIER); *G. Cissé*

"Deadline 2005 "
Med Biotech Laboratories (MBL) & Makerere Univ., Kampala; *T. G. Egwang, Jasper Ogwal-Okeng, George Lubega, David Okello*

"Développement durable et métropolisation à Ho Chi Minh City"
IREC-EPFL, Lausanne & Environmental Committee of Ho Chi Minh City (ENCO); *J.-C. Bolay, Bui thi Lang*

"Development of Molecular and Immunological Tools for the Diagnosis and Epidemiology of Foot and Mouth Disease"
Indian Veterinary Research Inst., Bangalore; Inst. of Biotechnology, ETH Zurich & Inst. of Virology & Immunoprophylaxis, Mittelhäusern; *C. Natarajan, G. Federspiel, K. Jenny, Ch. Griot*

"Dairy Cattle Health Control in Dar es Salaam Peri - Urban Animal Production Systems: An Example of Research Partnership"
Animal Disease Research Inst. (ADRI), Dar es Salaam & Bundesanstalt für Veterinärmedizin, Innsbruck; *A. M. Kapaga, K. C. Schoepf*

"Environmental protection measures in Galvanisation Plants in Ecuador"
Swisscontact & Swiss Foundation for Technical Co-operation, Zurich; Ingenieurschule beider Basel (IBB); *T. Heim*

"Environmental Technology Co-operation with Developing Countries. Environmental Technical Centre in Colombia"
Fed. Lab. for Material Testing & Research (EMPA), St. Gallen, ETHZ & Fed. Office for Foreign Economic Affairs (BAWI), Berne; *J. Gonzalez, C. Som, C. Edelmann, H.-P. Egler*

"Essential National Health Reasearch ENHR"
Council on Health Research for Development, COHRED, Geneva; *Y. Nuyens*

"Etude et essais d'amélioration de la conservation traditionelle de l'ignane (Dioscorea spp.) en Côte d'Ivoire"
Centre Suisse de Recherche Scientifique (CSRS) & Université d'Abidjan, Côte d'Ivoire & Department of Agriculture and Food Sciences ETHZ, Zurich; *Olivier Girardin, Charlemagne Nindjin, Domo Albert Otokoré, Zakaria Farah, Placide Zoungrana*

"Floods in Bangladesh"
Department of Geography, Univ. of Berne & Jahangirnagar Univ., Dhaka; *B. Messerli, T. Hofer, T. Hossain, S.M. Nurul Alam, A. Baquée*

"Fossil Water for Booming Mines in the Atacama Desert, Chile?"
Department of Geography, Universidad de Chile, Santiago; Department of Geography, Univ. of Berne; Department of Environmental Physics, Univ. of Berne & State Geological Survey Lower Saxony, Hannover, Germany; *H. Romero, Martin Grosjean, B. Messerli, Ueli Schotterer, Mebus A. Geyh*

Part IV   Poster Exhibition: List of Themes and Contact Persons

"Health Impact and Management of Wastewater Use in Small-Scale Agriculture in Urban Sahelian Settings: Risks and Potential Intervention Strategies"
Ecole inter-états d'ingénieurs de l'équipment rural (EIER), Ouagadougou; Swiss Tropical Inst. (STI), Basle; Office OMS, Nouakchott; EPFL, Lausanne; Centre régional pour l'eau potable et l'assainissment de faible coût (CREPA), Ouagadougou; *G. Cissé, P. Odermatt, M. Tanner, M. Lemine, C. Touré, L.Y. Maystre*

"Health Impact of Water and Sanitation Improvements in Rural Zimbabwe: A New Way Forward in Involving Communities in Self-Assessment"
Blair Research Laboratories (BRL), Ministry of Health Zimbabwe, Inst. of Water and Sanitation Development (IWSD), Harare; Swiss Tropical Inst. (STI), Basle; *T. Zhuwau, S. Musabayane, P. Taylor, S. Chandiwana, D. Mäusezahl, M. Tanner*

"Herbal Antimalarials in Current Traditional Treatment Practice: What Are Their Potentials?"
Ifakara Centre, Inst. of Med. Res. Kilombero, Tanzania; Swiss Tropical Inst., Univ. of Basle & Hoffmann la Roche, Basle; *C. Mlenge (Traditional Healer, Kilana, Tanzania), N. Hurt, A. Kitua, H. Mshinda, S. Hausmann, F. Matthies, M Tanner, U. Séquin, R. Ridley*

"How to Succeed in Plant Taxonomy in the Tropics? A Matter of Communication"
Universidad Nacional Experimental de Guayana, Upata, Estado Bolivar & Inst. de botanique, Univ. de Lausanne; *E. Sanoja, R. Keller*

"Limits to a Personal Medical North-South Contribution. 30 Years Intermittent Experience and its Relevance to the Workshop"
Swiss Serum and Vaccine Inst., Berne; *A. Poltera*

"Local Management of Forests as Determined by Environmental Perception and Traditional Knowledge in the Wider Himalayan Context"
Forest Policy and Forest Economics, ETHZ, Zurich; *Franz Schmithüsen, K Seeland*

"Mechanisms of Immunosuppression in Leprosy and Analysis of Mycobacterium leprae Genome"
Madurai Kamaraj Univ., India, Indo-Swiss Collaboration in Biotechnology (ISCB), Zurich, Univ. of Kaiserslautern & Univ. of Geneva; *K. Dharmalingam, VR. Muthukkaruppan, G. Federspiel, K. Jenny, J. Cullum, D. Hoessli*

"Methods for Diagnosis, Control and Prevention of Mycoplasmoses in Livestock"
Research Inst. for Animal Health, Wagholi, Inst. of Biotechnology, ETH Zurich, Inst. of Veterinary Bacteriology, Univ. of Berne; *S.N. Singh, S. Kilari, G. Federspiel, K. Jenny, J. Frey, J. Nicolet*

"Mycotoxin Contaminations of Food in Ecuador"
Inst. of Biochemistry, Univ. of Berne; *M. Mühlemann, Philipp Hübner, J. Lüthy*

"Operational Research as a Tool for the Promotion of Introduction of User Fees in Health Services in Tanzania"
Swiss Tropical Inst. (STI), Basle & Urban Health Project, Min. of Health, Dar es Salaam; *J. Rwezaura, K. Wyss, P. Kilama, F. Küchler, Maya Natarjan, Adiel Mushi, N. Lorenz*

"PAESI: Projet d'aménagement énergétique solaire intégré"
Laboratory for Industrial Energetics (LENI), EPF Lausanne; COGENER (Parc Scientifique & Tunis); Elektrowatt, Société Tunisienne de l'éléctricité et du Gaz (STEG); Agence pour la métrise de l'énergie (AME); Insitut national de recherche scientifique et technique (INRST), Tunisia; *D. Favrat, Y. Allani*

"Partnership with NARS in developing modules"
International Service for National Agricultural Research (ISNAR), The Hague; *Chr. Bonte-Friedheim*

Part IV Poster Exhibition: List of Themes and Contact Persons

"Postharvest Technology of Plantains"
Inst. of Food Science and Technology (LFO), ETH Zurich & IITA, Kampala, Univ. of Nigeria, Nsukka; *A. Ubi, F. Escher, Z. Farah, R.S.B. Ferris, N.D. Onwukka*

"Previsional Management of the Urban Environment: Public Policies and Local Dynamics in Intermediate Cities"
Inst. universitaire d'études du dév. (IUED), Inst. d'arch. de l'Univ. de Genève (IAUG) & Inst. d'urbanisme de Genève (IUG); *C. Mechkat, I. Milbert, Alain Viavio, Alicia Casalis et al.*

"Process-Based Research Capacity Building among Chadian Researchers and Civil Servants"
Swiss Tropical Inst. (STI), Basle & Bureau Appui Santé et Environment (BASE), Ministry of Public Health, N'Djamena; *K. Wyss, Emile Jeannée, Luc Cloutier, Ko lo Dingamnodij, Y. N'Dhiekor, Santa N'Dem, Mariam Alladoumugné*

"Promotion of Free Entreprises in Eastern Europe"
Vereinigung für freies Unternehmertum (vfu), Chur; *Markus Keller & J. Camenzind*

"Prospects for Academic Partnership and Research in African History. Opportunities for Joint Research Using a Collection of Historical Photographs in Basel."
Basel Mission Archive, Basle, Presbyterian Church in Cameroon & Protestant Chaplaincy, Univ. of Heidelberg; *Barbara Frey Näf, P. Jenkins, Jonas Dah*

"Research and Training in Reproductive Health"
WHO Collaborating Centre for Research in Human Reproduction & Univ. Hospital, Geneva; *Aldo Campana, Frank Lüdicke, E. Mathur*

"Research Partnership at the 'Centre Suisse de Recherche Scientifiques en Côte d'Ivoire'"
Académie Suisse des Sciences Naturelles (ASSN) & Ministère de l'Enseignement Supérieur de la Recherche et d'Innovation Technologique, Abidjan, Côte d'Ivoire; *J. Zinsstag, B.V. Onayogodé*

"SADAOC: A Regional Food Security Network in West Africa"
Inst. of Statistical, Social & Economic Research, Univ. of Ghana, Legon & European Centre for Development Policy Management (ECDPM), Maastricht; *Asenso Okyere, E. de Munck*

"Setting Research Priorities for the USAID"
USAID, Washington DC; *E. Augenbraun, F. E. Carr*

"Social and Political Dimensions of Environmental Programmes and Projects"
United Nations Research Inst. for Social Development (UNRISD), Geneva; Univ. Nacional de Costa Rica; Univ. of the Philippines, Los Baños; Ecole nationale d'économie appliquée, Senegal; Inst. Universitaire d'Etudes du Dév. (IUED), Geneva; Inst. of Geography, Univ. of Berne; Inst. of Geography, Univ. of Zurich; *P. Utting et al.*

"South-South Technology Transfer for Sustainable Development"
VACVINA, People's Committee of Tân Thanh, Isa of Ho Chi Minh City, Vietnam; Indian Inst. of Science, Bangalore; Fund for Renewable Energy - Decentralised (FREND), Seuzach; *N. Agustoni-Phan*

"Spatial Microhabitat selection by Biomphalaria pfeifferi in Mlali river, Tanzania"
Ifakara Centre, Ifakara, Postgraduate Course on Developing Countries (NADEL), ETH Zurich & Swiss Tropical Inst. (STI), Basle; *Charles Mayombana, Athumani Mtandanguo, Salehe Mtandanguo, J. Utzinger, M. Tanner*

Part IV   Poster Exhibition: List of Themes and Contact Persons

"Strategies and Activities"
Inst. of Biotechnology, ETH Zurich; *K. Jenny, G. Federspiel, B. Witholt*

"Sustainability for Future Generations. Gender Relations in Social Reproduction and Sustainable Resource Management"
Inst. for Ethnology, Univ. of Zurich & Society for International Development, Rome; *C. Wacker, Wendy Harcourt*

"Sustainable Activity"
Swiss Priority Programme Environment (SPPE), Berne; *R. Häberli*

"Technical Transfer and Training of Staff of the Livestock Health Research Institute (LIRI, Uganda) for Research Strengthening"
Swiss Tropical Inst. (STI), Basel; *R. Brun, R. Kaminsky*

"The 'Bureau d'Appui Santé et Environnement (BASE)' in Chad: A Platform for South-South and South-North Exchanges"
Swiss Tropical Inst. (STI), Basle & Bureau Appui Santé et Environment (BASE), N'Djamena; *Emile Jeannée, Ibni Oumar Mahamat Saleh, K. Wyss, Antoine Degrémont*

"The Egyptian-German Micronutrients Programme - A Case Study for North-South and South-South Research Cooperation for Sustainable Development"
Botany Department, National Research Centre, Cairo-Dokki, Egypt & Inst. for Plant Nutrition, TU München-Freising-Weihenstephan; *M.M. El-Fouly, A. Amberger*

"The Geochemistry, Vegetation and Zoology of a Tropical Swamp Forest in Central Kalimantan, Indonesia, and its Implications for Sustainable Development"
Geological Inst., Univ. of Berne; United States Geological Survey, Reston USA, Department of Life Sciences, Univ. of Nottingham UK; Department of Zoology, Univ. of Leicester, UK; Faculty of Agronomy, Univ. of Palangka Raya, Indonesia; East Midlands Environmental Consultants, Nottingham, UK; *D. Weiss, W. Shotyk, S.G. Neuzil, J. Rieley, S. Page, S. Limin, P. Shepard*

"The Indo-Swiss Biotechnology Programme (ISCB): Background, Organisation, Objectives and Tools"
Inst. of Biotechnology, ETH Zurich; *K. Jenny, G. Federspiel, B. Witholt*

"Towards Sustainable Development: An Actor-oriented Perspective. Strengthening Research Tools on Resource Management and Environment in South and Southeast Asia"
Inst. of Geography, Univ. of Zurich, Centre for Development Studies (CDS), Trivandrum; *U. Geiser, S. Wälty, A. Tarnutzer, R. Veron, M. Pronk, P.S. George, K.N. Nair, Paul Antonito, Jacob Jom, V. Govindaru, N.C. Narayanan*

"Tropical Biology Associations"
Inst. of Zoology, Univ. of Basle & Biological Sciences Building, Bristol; *S. Stearns, R. Trevelyan*

"Use and Protection of Water Resources in Lake Victoria through Sustainable Management of Wetland -Ecotopes"
Fisheries Research Inst., Jinja, Uganda, Pedagogic Univ. St. Gallen, Basel Inst. of Technology; Inst. for Social Anthropology and Inst. for Plant Biology, Univ. of Zurich, Zurich; *F.W.B. Bugenyi, John S. Balirwa, K. Frischknecht, H. Leuenberger, Agnes Nassuna, Henry Ocaya, Konstantine Odongkara, William Okello, Charles Olet-Ogwang, Grace Rupiny, C. Wacker, M. Wolf*

Part IV   Poster Exhibition: List of Themes and Contact Persons

"Water Supplies and Sanitation in Rural Zimbabwe: What are the Options for Health Impact Evaluations?"
STI, Basle, Inst. of Water and Sanitation Development (IWSD) & Blair Research Lab. (BRL), Harare; *D. Mäusezahl, M. Tanner, T. Zhuwau, S. Mtero, P. Taylor*

compiled by Daniel Maselli

Selected References touching the Domain of Research Partnership

Aldhous, P., Webb, J. 1995. Die Angst der Forscher vor den Partnern im Norden. In: FACTS 46/1995: 122.

Berthoud, G., Sitter-Liver, B. (eds.) 1996. The Responsible Scholar. Ethical Considerations in the Humanities and Social Sciences. Universitätsverlag Freiburg (Schweiz) & Watson Publishing, Canton MA.

Blaikie, P. 1995. Changing environment or changing views? A political ecology for developing countries. In: Geography 80, 3: 203-214.

Bouguerra, M.L. 1993. La recherche contre le Tiers-monde: multinationales et illusions du développement. PUF, Paris.

Bouthros-Ghali, B. 1995. An Agenda for Development. UN, New York

Brush, S. (ed.) 1996. Valuing Local Knowledge: indigenous people and intellectual property rights. Island Press, Washington DC.

Gibbons, M., Limoges, C., Novotny, H., Schwartzman, S., Scott, P., Trow, M. 1994. The new production of knowledge. The dynamics of science and research in contemporary societies. Sage Publications, London.

Gibbs, W.W. 1995. Lost Science in the Third World. In: Scientific American, August 1995: 76-83.

Graf, C., Zinkl, W.D. 1994. Die Förderung entwicklungsländer-relevanter Forschung und Entwicklung in der Schweiz. FER 145/1994. Schweizerischer Wissenschaftsrat, 3003 Berne.

Guyer, J., Richards, P. The Invention of Biodiversity: Social Perspectives on the Management of Biological Variety in Africa. In: Africa, 66, 1: 1-13.

Harcourt, W. (ed.), 1994: Feminist Perspectives on Sustainable Development. Society for International Development (SID) Rome & Zed Books Ltd. London / New Jersey.

Hountondji, P.J. 1994. Démarginaliser. In: Hountondji, P.J. (éd.) Les savoirs endogènes : pistes pour une recherche. CODESRIA, Dakar: 1-34.

Hountondji, P.J. 1996. Producing knowledge in Africa today. In: African Studies Review 38, 3: 1-10.

IUED 1996. Swiss Research in Developing Countries. Geneva.

Leisinger, K., Hösle, V. (Hg.) 1995. Entwicklung mit menschlichem Antlitz. Die Dritte und die Erste Welt im Dialog. Beck, München.

Messerli, B. 1995. Environment and Resources - Natural and Human Dimensions of "Global Change". In: Sitter-Liver B. and B. (eds.) Culture within Nature. Swiss Academy of Humanities and Social Sciences, Berne.

Morath, K. (Hg.) 1996. Welt im Wandel. Dauerhaft umweltgerechte Entwicklung als Herausforderung. Frankfurter Institut, Bad Homburg.

Oyen, E., Miller, S.M., Samad, S.A. (eds.) 1996. Poverty. A Global Review. A Handbook on International Poverty Research. UNESCO and Scandinavian University Press.

Pickering, A. (ed.) 1995. Science as Practice and Culture. Chicago Univ. Press, Chicago.

Prah, K. K. 1995. Mother Tongue for Scientific and Technological Development in Africa. German Foundation for Internat. Development, Bonn.

Raffer, K., Singer, H.W. (eds.) 1996. The Foreign Aid Business: Economic Assistance and Development Cooperation. Edgar Elgar, Aldershot.

Scheps, R. (éd.) 1993. La science sauvage : des savoirs populaires aux ethnosciences. Seuil, Paris.

Scoones, J, Thompson, J. (eds.) 1994. Beyond Farmers First: Rural people's knowledge, agricultural research and extension practice. IT Publications, London.

Smutylo, T, Koala, S. 1993. Research Networks, Evolution and Evaluation from a Donor's Perspective, IDRC, Ottawa (Canada).

Sottas, B. 1994. Problems and perspectives of scientific collaboration between Europe and Africa. In: Bearth, T., Möhlig, W., Sottas, B., Suter, E. (Hg.) Perspektiven afrikanistischer Forschung - Perspectives des recherches africanistes. Köppe, Köln: 379-402.

Taiwo, O. 1993. Colonialism and its aftermath: the crisis of knowledge production. In: Callaloo, Vol. 16, 3: 891-908.

Thulstrup, E.W. (ed.), Thulstrup, H.D. (assist. ed.), 1996: Research Training for Development - Proceedings of a Conference on Research Training for Countries with limited Research Capacity. Roskilde University Press

Thiel, R. (Hg.) 1996. Entwicklungspolitiken - 33 Geberprofile. Deutsches Übersee-Institut, Hamburg.

von der Meulen, B., Rip, A. 1994. Science Policy and Utilization of Research: Key Concepts and Insights. Centre for Studies of Science, Technology and Society; University of Twente (The Netherlands).